Praise for

'This is a smart, wise, well-written essay which answers with much common sense and learning one of the biggest questions of our time.'

Chris Patten, Chancellor of the University of Oxford and former Governor of Hong Kong

'An excellent, current guide to the challenges and dangers ahead for modern China. It describes, with verve and insight, why the "China Dream" may lead to a chilly awakening. Fenby, a delightful writer, explains why China will not dominate the 21st century with compelling critiques – and a sharp, clear summary of its economic and political challenges.'

Robert B. Zoellick, Former President of the World Bank Group, US Trade Representative and US Deputy Secretary of State

'Jonathan Fenby offers a well-informed and balanced assessment of China's past and prospects, recognising its remarkable economic achievements but also noting the huge economic, social and political challenges it confronts. China will not, he concludes, dominate the world in the 21st century. He is almost certainly right.'

Martin Wolf, Chief Economics Commentator, *The Financial Times*

'An excellent summary of the broad spectrum of very serious issues China faces in the immediate future.'

Fraser Howie, author of *Red Capitalism: The Fragile Financial Foundation of China's Extraordinary Rise*

Population decline + life expectancy

'Jonathan Fenby has managed a highly impressive feat: within a short and elegant text, he has pinpointed the real challenges facing China today if it is truly to become a global actor that will play a serious role in the coming century. The insights give us a road-map for what we might expect from this superpower in the making. A compelling and essential read from a premier China analyst.'

Rana Mitter, author of *China's War with Japan, 1937–1945: The Struggle for Survival*

'China is a bubble in multiple ways – not least in the way its supposed never-ending rise is interpreted and understood in the West. Jonathan Fenby shows courage and insight in pricking the bubble in this important book.'

Will Hutton, *Observer* columnist and author of *The Writing on the Wall*

'Fenby's thoughtful, balanced analysis of what China has achieved, how it has done so, and the challenges ahead is an excellent corrective to the surfeit of overly laudatory and excessively dire assessments of China's future and its implications for the world.'

Thomas Fingar, Stanford University

'In this spirited and insightful book, Jonathan Fenby takes on the China bulls by taking a clear-eyed look at China's dysfunctional political system, which does not appear up to the task of tackling the social, legal, economic, environmental, demographic and security challenges facing the country. Highly recommended.'

Joseph Fewsmith, Boston University, author of *The Logic and Limits of Political Reform in China*

Will China Dominate the 21st Century?

Global Futures Series

Jonathan Fenby

WILL CHINA DOMINATE THE 21st CENTURY?

Second edition

polity

First edition published in 2014 by Polity Press
This edition published in 2017 by Polity Press

Polity Press
65 Bridge Street
Cambridge CB2 1UR, UK

Polity Press
350 Main Street
Malden, MA 02148, USA

ISBN-13: 978-1-5095-1096-2
ISBN-13: 978-1-5095-1097-9 (pb)

A catalogue record for this book is available from the British Library.

Library of Congress Cataloging-in-Publication Data

Names: Fenby, Jonathan, author.
Title: Will China dominate the 21st century? / Jonathan Fenby.
Description: Second edition. | Cambridge, UK ; Malden, MA : Polity Press, 2017. | Series: Global futures series | Includes bibliographical references.
Identifiers: LCCN 2016033699 (print) | LCCN 2016035279 (ebook) | ISBN 9781509510962 (hardback) | ISBN 9781509510979 (pbk.) | ISBN 9781509510986 (Epdf) | ISBN 9781509510993 (Mobi) | ISBN 9781509511006 (Epub)
Subjects: LCSH: China--History--21st century. | China--Economic conditions--2000- | China--Politics and government--21st century.
Classification: LCC DS779.4 .F47 2017 (print) | LCC DS779.4 (ebook) | DDC 303.4951--dc23
LC record available at https://lccn.loc.gov/2016033699

Typeset in 11 on 15 pt Sabon by
Servis Filmsetting Ltd, Stockport, Cheshire
Printed and bound in Great Britain by CPI Group (UK) Ltd, Croydon

For further information on Polity, visit our website:
politybooks.com

Contents

1

The China Dream

With an economy set to be the biggest on earth in a few years, the world's largest population, an expanding global presence, a modernizing military and an assertively nationalistic one-party regime, China may well seem bound to dominate the present century. Stretching across 3.7 million square miles (99.6 million square kilometres) from the East China Sea to Central Asia, from the Siberian border to the semi-tropical south-west, it has become a major motor of international production and commerce, with an ever-increasingly international political presence as the main beneficiary of globalization.

Rich in people but poor in resources, its high level of demand is the main force in the global trade in commodities, ranging from iron ore to peanuts, determining the fortunes of countries in Africa,

Australia, Brazil and elsewhere in Asia. The speed and scale of its material renaissance are unequalled. Annual real growth has been above 8 per cent in all but eight of the past 35 years; when it dropped below that level in 2015–16, it was still far greater than that of other major nations.

Four decades ago, the People's Republic of China (PRC) was heading for basket-case status at the end of the Mao Zedong era; now it breeds super-latives and world leaders beat a path to its door. Everything seems bigger in the one-time Middle Kingdom than anywhere else – from mega-cities and super computers to its space programmes and even the huge industry in counterfeit goods and the online trolls who post half-a-billion fake social media messages each year. Though 150 million people still lived on less than $2 a day by the World Bank's measurement in 2010, another 600 million had lifted themselves out of poverty in the first three decades of growth. The most extensive infrastruc-ture development ever seen, which was ratcheted up by the huge stimulus programme launched at the end of 2008, has included laying the longest high-speed rail network in record time, constructing the enormous Three Gorges Dam on the Yangtze River and threading the country with airports, multi-lane highways and soaring bridges.[1]

After centuries of semi-seclusion and isolation from the main global currents under Mao, China now bestrides the world stage; its leader, Xi Jinping, made 14 state visits in 2015. The PRC disburses hundreds of billions of dollars in aid and investment around the globe and has taken initiatives designed to rival the (US) dollar-led post-1945 global order as it pursues what its President dubs the 'China Dream' of national rejuvenation and world respect.

While the United States frets about maintaining its world role, China exhibits no such doubts and sees itself moving into the vacuum as *Pax Sinica* succeeds *Pax Americana*. As a global superpower, the PRC holds a permanent seat on the United Nations (UN) Security Council and possesses nuclear arms. Its currency is widely used in global commerce; the International Monetary Fund (IMF) took the renminbi into its Special Drawing Rights (SDR) system in 2016. It is the economic leader among developing nations, the cornerstone of the BRICS grouping (Brazil, Russia, India, China and South Africa) and the moving force behind the new Asian Infrastructure Investment Bank (AIIB). It plans to breathe life into a new version of the Silk Road with assistance totalling tens of billions of dollars. It has the largest standing army on earth and is the biggest contributor of troops to UN peace-keeping forces. An array of foreign nations, from Britain to Uzbekistan, are anxious for its favours, as they showed in 2015 by resisting US advice not to join the AIIB.

China's performance since Mao's successor, Deng Xiaoping, unleashed economic expansion and connected his country with the world has led to widespread forecasts that the PRC will, according to one book title, 'rule the world' as the influence of the last major Communist Leninist state takes over from the West and the globe 'becomes more Chinese'. What has been achieved since the late 1970s is taken to mean that the 21st century must belong to the People's Republic since, in the words of the historian Niall Ferguson in 2011, 'for the next 10 or 20 years it is going to be very hard to derail China's economic locomotive'. Its history and civilization are held to give it advantages which the West cannot match. It is said to be run by a uniquely capable meritocracy that provides wise, long-term rule which eludes messy democratic governments.[2]

This book posits, on the contrary, that, spectacular as its growth and emergence on to the world stage have been, the PRC is hidebound by a set of factors which will limit its progress, some new and some reaching back into the distant past. This is not to say, however, that China will implode – forecasts of its coming collapse voiced since the start of this century have proved wrong and will continue to be mistaken. The country has too many assets and too much remaining potential for growth for that to happen. Its ruling caste will use everything at its disposal to ward off trouble and maintain its supremacy – a short-term defensive attitude which is at the root of many of the difficulties surrounding the Xi administration.

Rather than ruling the world or collapsing, the PRC will be caught in the limitations of its one-party system and the power apparatus on which the regime is founded. Attention is usually focused on the economy, with the perpetuation of the monopoly Party State which has ruled since the Communists won the civil war against the Kuomintang Nationalists in 1949 taken as a given. But it is the politics of China that are the determining factor, as they have been throughout its history.

Today, the confines of the political system and the over-riding need of the leaders to cling on to power on behalf of the Communist Party make it virtually impossible for them to address adequately the array of challenges before them, many the result of politically motivated mismanagement of the growth process that so impresses the world. They know that the era of turbo-charged growth is past: most observers doubt the official growth figures for 2015–16, referred to above, which show annual expansion slowing to 6.5–7 per cent, believing that the true figure is even lower. What counts is the leadership's ability to manage that decline in an increasingly challenging international context of contracting global commerce. This will involve political choices, and all the signs are that these will be constrained by the power imperatives driving Xi Jinping and his administration.

As a result, the outcome is likely to be summed up in a phrase not usually associated with the PRC: 'muddling through'. This conclusion will disappoint those who seek a sharp, headline-grabbing vision of the future. But it is set to be the reality as the conflicting priorities of Xi and his colleagues inhibit them. As a result, rather than achieving the 'China Dream', the PRC appears headed for a Middle Development Trap in which it will not fulfil its promise, because the political system prevents it from taking the initiatives and risks needed to attain its full potential.

There is nothing new in the awe China inspires – or in the qualifications which need to be attached to it. The rulers of the Middle Kingdom have always spun narratives of uniqueness and power to impress their own people and establish their nation's superiority for foreigners. They have sought to assume sweeping, supra-human dimensions as they guide a land which they class not as a country like others, but one whose destinies are protected by the Mandate of Heaven. Barbarian admirers have ranged from Marco Polo to Voltaire – though Napoleon's celebrated remark that the world would tremble when China awoke showed that he had not appreciated that the dragon was far from asleep, coming as it did just at the point at which the Qing dynasty was extending the frontiers of a nation that accounted for perhaps one-third of global wealth.

In our time, those let down by the failure of the Soviet Union to survive the Cold War invest their hopes in a new and formidable challenger to America. Those who doubt the efficacy of democracy and prefer the smack of firm government look with favour on a system that has no time for competitive elections, stamps on dissent and preaches discipline. Enthusiasts for Asia as the region which will shape the world are predisposed to cheer its largest power. Anti-colonialists see Beijing as a champion of their camp. Free marketers can close their eyes to the incantations of Marxism as they herald the opportunities offered by the last great business frontier where regulation, labour laws and environmental rules are agreeably flexible.

These reasons for admiration contain significant flaws, just as the imperial dynasties were frequently less impressive than they appeared. China is still a long way from achieving equal status with the United States in terms of economic strength, military might or innovation. Indeed, Chinese think tanks analysing the fall of the USSR have pointed to the dangers of getting into a knock-down competition with the power across the Pacific. The absence of debate and the strengthening of dogmatic rule under Xi Jinping are a recipe for stagnation; Taiwan's evolution as a democracy in this century stands in striking contrast to the authoritarian system imposed on the mainland. Though they welcome the benefits offered by the economic growth of China, most Asian nations are alarmed at its power projection and want to go on sheltering under the strategic umbrella Washington has offered East Asia since 1945. The military occupation of Tibet and the huge western territory of Xinjiang looks like a major exercise of colonial rule. As for Chinese business, it can be far from a straightforward market exercise on a level playing field as personal contacts, political interference and corner-cutting come into play in the absence of a reliable and independent legal system. Surveys in 2016 by Western Chambers of Commerce in the PRC reported growing pessimism among their members about doing business on the mainland in an 'increasingly hostile' environment deterring increased investment.[3]

The ancient Confucian civilization which writers like Martin Jacques see as central to their argument that China will come to rule the world has certainly left a powerful legacy, but one may ask how relevant it is to the question at hand, since it offers little or nothing in the way of answers to the present challenges facing the PRC. The sage from Shandong, after all, ranked merchants at the bottom of his social scale. Mao waged a relentless war against his teachings and, in today's China, the 'ism' that rules is materialism, epitomized by the young woman on a television dating show who said she would 'rather cry in the back of a BMW than laugh on the back of a bicycle'.

When it comes to the assertion that the world will become 'more Chinese' and that Chinese influence will spread its soft power through the globe, a stroll through any mainland city and its equivalent in Europe or America will show which culture is the more influential. There are not many Mao suits or Chinese films in Birmingham, England, or Birmingham, Alabama, but Chinese wear jeans, flock to Hollywood films and lap up *Downton Abbey*. On the mainland, people eat at fast food restaurants on the pattern of KFC and McDonald's; prime time shows on state television follow foreign patterns; Chinese car models ape those from the West and Japan; and Alibaba has become a monster online enterprise by adapting Western technology and techniques to the domestic market. An international survey in 2016 put the PRC in only 29th place among nations in the soft power league, while official data showed that the number of Chinese students going to foreign universities rose by 14 per cent in 2015 to 523,700.[4] Indeed, the degree of popular cultural influence from the West, Japan and South Korea is such that, in 2016, the State Council issued an order banning media from running stories which might promote it further.

History has always been a tricky matter in China, since it is shaped to the political imperatives of those in authority. The picture of a glorious imperial age has to be tempered by less glorious realities: recurrent disunion; civil wars; the violent overthrow of rulers; military incursions that led to two foreign dynasties; natural disasters; the refusal to adopt 19th-century modernization; and humiliation at the hands of the Japanese. The next century brought further misery: a decade of national warlord anarchy after the fall of the Empire; weak and largely reactionary Nationalist government; fresh invasions by Japan from 1931 to 1945; a massive toll in deaths and destruction; four years of civil war; and then the traumas of the Mao era from 1949 to 1976, culminating in famine which killed more than 40 million people, many as a result of official policies and bungling.

The vast National History Museum in Beijing leaves no doubt about how the past is to be interpreted. The 'century of humiliation' narrative is laid out so as to place the blame for China's decline in the 19th century squarely on foreigners, rather than on the internal divisions that sapped imperial authority on a much bigger scale. Pre-1949 events are tailored to show that the coming to power of the Communists was an inevitable process, and Mao is treated as a godlike figure who may have made mistakes but who is officially judged as having been '70 per cent good, 30 per cent bad'. He remains the core figure of the Communist Party State: his embalmed body visited by crowds in its mausoleum in Tiananmen Square in the middle of Beijing, his face on all banknotes, the Lenin and Stalin of the PRC rolled into one – a figure about whom the truth cannot be told for fear that it would undermine the regime over whose creation he presided.

The suppression of dissent in Beijing on 4 June 1989 has to be swept under the carpet, while the protests that were crushed on that day are dismissed as a counter-revolutionary plot by 'black hands' serving foreign interests seeking to bring down the PRC. The fact that most of those who died that night were ordinary citizens of the capital machine-gunned from the tanks on the avenue leading to the square is not something the regime can acknowledge. More than a quarter of a century after the massacre, mothers who commemorate their sons killed on 4 June are harassed and student leaders remain in exile.

History is thus rewritten – and, when necessary, created – to serve political needs. In September 2015, a grand military parade was held in Beijing over which Xi Jinping presided in his role as head of the People's Liberation Army (PLA). The occasion was organized to celebrate the seventieth anniversary of the defeat of Japan and the PLA occupied centre stage. But its contribution to the outcome in 1945 was minimal. China had waited for the United States to win the war, and most of the fighting on the mainland had been done by the Kuomintang forces while the Communists kept their powder dry for the civil war that would follow. No matter; China was embroiled in a territorial quarrel with Japan and the past was presented in such a way as to buttress nationalist sentiment.[5]

The belief that today's rulers are selected by a rigorous meritocratic process which gives them an unusually high level of sagacity hardly stands up to examination. The Communist Party congresses of 2007 and 2012 which propelled Xi to the summit as General Secretary of the Communist Party, State President and head of the military were occasions for intense politicking, which will be described in the next chapter. Factions and interest groups have thrived in the century so far; in 2016, Xi identified 'cliques and cabals' as 'compromising the political security of the party and the country'.[6]

For fear of shaking the social stability which the regime so prizes, the leadership fights shy of change and often adopts short-term fixes worthy of the most voter-driven democratic politicians. During the years of plenty in the first decade of this century, China's leaders failed to introduce reforms needed to turn the cheap-labour, cheap-capital, high-export economy born in the 1980s into something more sustainable and better balanced. When the global financial crisis hit in 2008, the government in Beijing vastly over-reacted with an expansion of credit that ended up by flooding the system with ten times the amount of money needed for the infrastructure stimulus programme; the hangover still affects the economy. More recently, the Xi administration has mishandled policy initiatives on the stock market and the currency amid policy confusion and diminishing international confidence.

The Party leaders profess to want to 'harness the dynamism of the market'; but their actions show that they do not understand how markets work. Nor are they ready to relax the control urge that has always been at the core of the Communist DNA to allow the liberalization necessary to advance the economy and meet the demands of an evolving society. The quality of the senior technocrats, many educated abroad, is often high and impresses prophets of meritocracy, but, as one senior academic in Beijing put it, 'China is run by smart people doing the wrong thing'.[7]

Xi and his colleagues know that the economy, whose health gives the regime its legitimacy in the absence of elections, the rule of law and public accountability, needs serious structural reform, but they also know that such change would impede growth in the short term and threaten the vested interests of the state over which they preside. This is not simply a matter of protecting state-owned enterprises (SOEs) and the fortunes amassed by well-connected people in the era of turbo-charged expansion. The risk aversion reaches much deeper. The fear in a system where everything connects under the aegis of the Party is that removing one brick could bring the whole edifice crashing down. The example of the Soviet Union is much cited; in one of his early speeches as Communist General Secretary, Xi said that the collapse of the USSR had come about because, when the test came, there had been no strong figure to defend the system. His whole trajectory since reaching the top at the end of 2012 has been to make himself the protector the Soviet system lacked and to ensure that the Party is sufficiently resilient to ward off any dangers that confront it.

If that means caution on reform, so be it. But caution spells trouble in the medium to long term as the PRC fails to evolve in ways that maximize its potential. Hence the prospect of the Middle Development Trap, as a once-revolutionary regime turns conservative under a centralized authoritarian elite that cannot relax its grip or escape from the political-economic nexus which lay at the heart of Deng's policy but which now threatens to strangle his successors as they hang on to the past while needing to move into the future.

The patriarch's purpose after he emerged victorious from the power struggle that followed

Mao's death in 1976 was primarily political. The economic drive which astounded the world was pursued because it served a deeper purpose.

Deng was three things: a Chinese patriot; a faithful Communist since joining the Party as a teenager in France in the 1920s; and a believer in ruthless power politics, as he had shown with his repression of alleged class enemies at Mao's behest after the victory of 1949. He wanted to make China a great power again after the catastrophes inflicted on it by the Great Helmsman and to rebuild the Party from the near-terminal damage Mao had wreaked upon it during the Cultural Revolution, when Deng had been among the members of the hierarchy who were purged. He saw that these aims could be achieved through economic growth at a time of strong export demand abroad and the lowering of tariff barriers in the onward march of globalization. Where Mao had changed his nation by leading the Communists to victory, Deng changed the world by unleashing abundant cheap labour and cheap capital from savings to produce low-range goods to meet global demand as China opened up on an unprecedented scale.

The result has constituted the most significant global development since the end of the Cold War. China's gross domestic product (GDP) rocketed to reach $11 trillion by 2015 in terms of currency prices; evaluated by purchasing power parity, which measures what money can actually buy, that number expands to $19 trillion, ahead of America's. In 2016, China counted more dollar billionaires than the United States. For the first time in its history, it has also nurtured a sizeable middle class, which has become a major driver of global consumption, affecting the fortunes of exporters of everything from high-end luxury goods to more mundane products.[8]

Chinese companies seem to buy up foreign firms and assets by the week, from mineral reserves to American cinema chains; in the first half of 2016, they announced overseas deals worth $107 billion, often benefiting from cheap state finance. The Sinopec oil and gas group claims to be the biggest joint platform operator in the North Sea, while PRC firms have helped to bankroll Brazil's sub-salt off-shore energy exploration. China offers to build high-speed rail network and other infrastructure in countries across the globe.

While the great goal is to achieve equality with the United States, the PRC is, more immediately, bent on establishing superiority by pressing its claims to sovereignty over most of the South China Sea and getting the better of its old enemy, Japan.

These confrontations have wide-ranging implications. The South China Sea is the main maritime route for traded goods and Asian imports of oil and other raw materials, as well as being a rich fishing ground and containing energy reserves below the sea bed. When they met in California in 2013, Xi told President Obama that the Pacific was big enough for both of their countries, meaning that the Americans should move their forces back across the ocean from Okinawa to Guam. That would remove the post-1945 American strategic umbrella from a part of the world which is a major component of the global economy. As if this was not enough, commentary on the big military parade in Beijing in 2015 warned that the PRC had missiles that could reach the US military base in Guam.[9]

Internationally and at home, Xi Jinping stands out in a world where strong leadership of big, economically powerful countries has become rare. Holder of a dozen top posts ranging through the Communist Party, the state, the military and the economy, he is the centre of a personality cult which conveys quasi-imperial status as leader of a nation that sees itself as existing on a plane of its own with little or no need of a global order shared with other nations. The 'princeling' son of a first-generation Communist leader is the most powerful hands-on leader the country has known since Mao. The big anti-corruption campaign he launched on taking the Party leadership has enabled him to bring down real or potential rivals and to get away from the factionalism and need for consensus that weakened his predecessor, Hu Jintao. His second term in office will last until 2022, and it is likely that he will seek to influence his successors after that – unless he decides to break precedence by extending his time at the top beyond the usual two terms.

The Communist Party he heads has no rivals for power (if only because it has eliminated them) and is the world's biggest political organization with 87 million members – which is equalled by the membership of its Youth League, though this is likely to be reduced in a drive to make the latter a tighter, more efficient outfit under stricter control from the centre. The economics-led political and social stability the Party has enforced since the death of Mao in 1976 contrasts sharply with the convulsions of the previous century-and-a-half, providing a narrative which has become a fetish for the rulers as they stamp out any form of competition or opposition, be it from non-governmental organizations, human rights lawyers, websites or figures such as Liu Xiaobo, the 2010 Nobel Peace Prize Winner, in jail for 11 years for advocating democracy.

Such factors may appear to buttress the case for China's coming dominance in a world in which the other superpower is looking increasingly inward and Western doubts contrast with the confidence shown by the leadership in Beijing. However, again, this is to overlook major qualifications that need to be considered.

The repression and dogmatism which the Xi administration regards as essential for regime preservation run counter to the aspirations of a rapidly evolving society. The bargain offered to the population after the bloody suppression of protests in 1989, namely material growth in return for abstinence from politics, is coming under growing strain as crude increases in overall wealth cut less ice with the second-generation urban middle class. They worry more than their parents did about the lack of effective action against rampant pollution, which cuts life expectancy in northern cities by 5.5 years, makes 80 per cent of water from wells unsafe to drink and poisons farmland with pesticides and heavy metal deposits. The trust deficit with a detached ruling elite dedicated to the preservation of monopoly power is becoming too wide to be bridged by propaganda in an age of social media. Citizens are told to have confidence in the Party hierarchy and to follow nostrums handed down by the leadership, but a popular jibe advises people to believe something only when the rulers deny it.

This gulf is exacerbated by public exasperation at quality-of-life issues. Water is growing critically short in the north. Food safety is a major concern, heightened by scandals such as the putrid meat being used by a big sausage manufacturer, contaminated mineral water and the lacing of milk used for baby formula and other dairy products with dangerously high levels of the industrial chemical melamine. The growth of major cities has made them uncomfortable places in which to live for most people except the mega-rich. A big expansion of university education has produced millions of unemployed graduates each year, posing the classic problems of a country with too many educated young people without jobs. The materialism fostered by economic growth, the fraying of ideology and the promotion of consumerist goals has left a spiritual void in which Christianity has attracted millions. This has led to a contest between the religious affairs administration, which seeks to control churches and appoint bishops, and Catholics, who look to the Vatican as the legitimate source of spiritual leadership.

The demographics are going the wrong way.

After benefiting from an influx of young workers into the labour force during the first generation of development, the PRC now faces the impact of a significantly lower growth rate, caused by falling fertility and the one-child policy. At the same time, improved health care has raised life expectancy in a society where the state makes little provision for the old and pensions are inadequate. The easing of the one-child policy in 2015 will take a long time to have an impact, and initial signs are that couples do not want to have a lot of children because of the cost of raising them, particularly in cities, where kindergartens are hugely over-subscribed and parents worry about the effect of bad air on the throats and lungs of their offspring.

Internationally, the assertion of imperial-era pretensions unnerves East Asian countries which may share a Confucian heritage but have no desire to be dictated to and which value their American security connections. In trying simultaneously to over-awe and court them, China exhibits a strange combination of superiority and victimhood as it cites past suffering at the hands of foreigners as a justification for asserting its authority. The result has been that a normally quiescent country like the Philippines felt emboldened to go to a UN arbitration tribunal in 2016 to complain about the PRC's expansion in the South China Sea. The reaction from Beijing was telling. Rather than arguing its case at the internal body, the PRC shunned the hearings and announced in advance that any verdict would be null and void since its sovereignty claim was sacrosanct. Having based its claim over most of the 1.3 million square mile (3.5 million square kilometre) sea on a map of unclear provenance dating from 1947, Beijing then referred to an ancient notebook it said proved its case, though this foundered when its supposed owners said it had not been preserved. None of this reassured other countries about working with the PRC in what was widely regarded as a test case of Beijing's readiness to live by international rules. Calls for China to act as a 'responsible global stakeholder' met with no response, and when the UN tribunal finally ruled against it, Beijing simply refused to take any notice. Meanwhile, countries of South-East Asia drew closer to the United States as their protector, with Vietnam hosting President Obama in 2016 and Washington agreeing to sell arms to its former adversary.

The negative impact for China of its power projection and the limits on Beijing's strategic influence are evident round East Asia. The PRC's insistence on pushing a dispute with Japan over a group of uninhabited islands accompanied by naval and aerial probing has encouraged the government in Tokyo to move away from the post-war policy of non-militarization. North Korea's pursuit of its nuclear ambitions has embarrassingly shown Beijing's inability to impose itself on its 'Little Brother' across the Yalu River. For all the drive to modernize the PLA, American naval and air units based in south Japan remain the most powerful military force in Asia. While the United States has treaty alliances with Japan, South Korea and the Philippines and it also has close relations with other countries such as Singapore, the PRC avoids commitments with other countries, which it expects to accept tributary-state status to the reborn Middle Kingdom.

Hong Kong and the island of Taiwan present particular problems. The former, which returned to Chinese sovereignty in 1997, has been subject to a toughening of Beijing's policy and intervention in its affairs, which has led to push-back from protesters insisting that the 'one country, two systems' formula decreed at the handover means that the PRC should stay out of the running of the former colony. This is not something Beijing relishes, and it has shown diminishing respect for the autonomy of the Special Administrative Region (SAR) set up on Britain's departure. This was exemplified by

Beijing's ominous reaction to one particular case of criticism. When a Hong Kong bookseller and publisher put out accounts containing insider information about Chinese leaders in 2015, five of the company's employees were abducted to the mainland. After his release, together with three of the other detainees (their colleague Gui Minhai remains in custody at the time of writing), Lam Wing Kee said he had been interrogated more than 20 times, with questioning centring on books that touched on Xi and his private life.[10]

Though reunited with the PRC, inhabitants of the former colony regard themselves as different from mainlanders – polls regularly show that a big majority regard themselves not simply as 'Chinese' but as 'Hong Kong Chinese' or 'Hongkongers'. With its rule of law, tradition of free speech and taste for protest erupting in the 'Umbrella Revolution' of 2014 against greater mainland control, Hong Kong is going to be hard for Beijing to bring into line, and, as such, provides a striking reflection of the limitations of the China model. (The former Portuguese colony of Macau across the bay is less of a problem, being politically subservient and dependent on gambling revenue.)

Ever since Chiang Kai-shek led Nationalist forces to Taiwan in 1949 after their defeat in the civil war with the Communists, Beijing has regarded the island as a 'renegade province' which must be reunited with the mainland, by force if necessary. But since Chiang's son began to dismantle the dictatorship of the Kuomintang party following his father's death in 1975, Taiwan has emerged as a democracy which does not want to return to the fold and hopes it has a security guarantee from the United States. Attempts by the PRC to intimidate and then to beguile the island and its 23 million people have fallen flat. A charm offensive launched in 2008 offering economic agreements failed to prevent the autonomist-minded Democratic Progressive Party from sweeping the board at presidential and legislative elections eight years later. Faced with the failure of its policies, Beijing has to decide whether to accept the reality of the island's desire to live its own life or whether to brandish the threat of its force of more than a thousand missiles positioned across the 100-mile Taiwan Strait.

For all this, growth and growing global importance have bred commensurate self-confidence and boosted nationalism in the PRC. Those who point to problems are cast as subversives, in keeping with the way in which dissent has tended to be equated with treason throughout the country's history. This bred a degree of complacency after the burst of reform undertaken before the PRC's entry into the World Trade Organization in 2001. While officials will acknowledge problems in private, and, very occasionally, in public, too, the over-riding mind-set this century has been that everything will turn out right because it has always done so, because the Communist Party knows what it is doing, and because this is China, and China is a special place with a special destiny. Again, there is precedent for this attitude.

Under the four-decade ascendancy of the Dowager Empress Cixi, which ended with her death in 1908, the court in the Forbidden City rejected change until its very last gasp; attempts to recast Cixi as a reformer are unconvincing. The 'Self-strengtheners', who pioneered industrialization in the later 19th century, were a small band whose enterprises were swamped by the dominance of agriculture, the conservativism of the Confucian gentry and Cixi's concern to preserve the rule of her non-Chinese Manchu dynasty and its circle. In what the historian Mark Elvin has called the 'high-level equilibrium trap',[11] steady growth in farm output disguised the need for change in China's operating methods and the development of new fields of activity.

Such a shift would have presented dangers for the deeply conservative political system; when one emperor tried it after the catastrophic defeat by Japan in 1894–5, he was quickly reined in by the Dowager, having sabotaged his own initiative by trying to do too much too fast and by enlisting an adviser from Tokyo. At the turn of the century, Cixi and her court once more displayed their obtuseness by allying with the anti-foreign Boxer Rising. This brought another major disaster down on the dynasty, which had only a dozen years to go before rebellion broke out and Cixi's successor as Dowager agreed to the abdication of the infant Last Emperor after the regime's main commander turned against it, anti-Manchu feeling exploded and the empire of 2,100 years crumbled, the victim of its own short-sightedness and overweening pride.

If that saga provides obvious warnings for a similarly self-confident regime of today, there are other elements in the past that raise questions over the assertion that Chinese civilization provides a unique key to future strength. Without denying the size and longevity of the imperial system, as a land-based entity, China failed to exploit maritime power, except for a brief period in the early 15th century. It was never a global force, being constricted to East Asia and parts of Central Asia, and never had anything like the international impact of Britain,

Spain, Portugal, France, the Netherlands or, later, the United States and the Soviet Union.

Confucianism is held to have been a compassionate lodestar for Chinese civilization with its teaching that one should act towards others as one would wish them to act towards oneself. But the behaviour pattern it advocates, which holds that children should show filial piety to their father in return for his benevolence towards them, promotes a top-down relationship in which it is the father who defines the benevolence he accords and the offspring who have to be satisfied with showing obedient piety. Translated into political terms, this is an obviously attractive creed for autocrats, particularly when it lays such stress on rituals and social hierarchies – everything in its place, like shoes and hats, as a faithful 19th-century Confucian military commander said while his forces slaughtered peasant rebels.

The imperial civil service chosen by rigorous examination is presented as having produced an unrivalled administrative meritocracy which is perpetuated to this day. But the length and complexity of the education required to pass the tests meant that successful candidates came mainly from rich and scholarly families – moreover, in the late imperial period, degrees could be bought or were given in return for service. Nor did meritocracy extend to the rulers: emperors took the throne by inheritance or violence.

The diplomacy of the late imperial period, whereby China's foes were meant to be set against each other, is regarded by admirers such as Henry Kissinger as the acme of subtle, encircling statecraft, in contrast to the crude frontal approach of the West.[12] But, however elegantly expressed in theory, in practice it brought the late Qing little success, as barbarians failed to fight among themselves and repeatedly humbled the Middle Kingdom. There is also a myth that China was not an expansionist power and was content to exist within its settled borders. So what of imperial campaigns against the Uyghurs, Kazakhs, Kyrgyzs, Evenks and Mongols and invasions of Vietnam, Korea and Burma? And what of the fact that, in the early years of the People's Republic, the army went into Tibet and Xinjiang, which have remained part of China ever since, with their large non-Han populations and high levels of ethnic tension?

Top-down rule and political opacity have a very long history in China. Occasional forecasts from scattered foreign commentators that there is bound to be a move towards Western-style democracy appear to be based on extrapolation from elsewhere and wishful thinking about the middle class. The essential prerequisite of the independent rule of law has always been missing and there is no tradition of peaceful competition for office. China has held just one quasi-democratic election – after the fall of the Qing in 1912; the leader of the winning party was assassinated immediately afterwards and a military strongman took over. Village elections have been introduced in recent years, but they are tightly controlled, with candidates regarded as unsuitable by the authorities being barred from standing. Selections of delegates to the annual plenary session of the national legislature are equally vetted, while the selection of members of the Communist Party Politburo and its all-powerful Standing Committee takes place behind closed doors in utmost secrecy.

Openness has always been regarded as dangerous, by emperors of the past and today's Communist Party alike. This not only rules out political reform but also affects the key area of the economy, the basis of the regime's claim to legitimacy. The closed system which rulers have always preferred militates against the adoption of new approaches and methods appropriate to changing circumstances. For all its impressive achievements, the PRC thus remains true to the nation's past, stuck in ways of thinking dictated both by the legacy of its civilization and by the leadership's fear of losing power. Self-preservation of this kind comes at a heavy cost and is the principal reason why China will not dominate our century.

2

The Price of Politics

The era of Xi Jinping, which began at the end of 2012, has been marked by increased imposition of central political power from the top as a return to rule by a single dominant individual has replaced the consensus leadership seen under his predecessor, Hu Jintao. That might point to a consolidation of authority to reinforce the stability the regime seeks. Almost certainly, Xi sees it that way. But the reality is that it heightens the risk factor in China, spreading beyond the Communist Party arena to affect the economy, society and the military as the leadership style becomes increasingly totalitarian. The fundamental problem is that the nature of the PRC after nearly four decades of development means the Xi approach is unlikely to work, either in his own terms or in promoting the evolution of the nation as a whole.

Xi's ascent to the array of senior posts he now holds as chief of the fifth generation of Communist leaders was a methodical process during which he came to identify himself with the Party to the extent that he could claim to embody its best interests. He began with an important historical inheritance. His father, Xi Zhongxun, was a military commander during the civil war with the Nationalists and was appointed as a vice-premier under Mao, making his son a member of the regime's 'princeling' aristocracy. The elder Xi was purged during the Cultural Revolution, following which his son was sent from his elite school in Beijing to the northern countryside to live in a cave and look after pigs. His attempts to join the Communist Party were rebuffed, and he has recalled the upheaval of the last decade of Mao's life as 'emotional ... a mood ... an illusion'.[1] When his father was rehabilitated by Deng and put in overall charge of the spearhead economic development province of Guangdong, the younger Xi became secretary to a prominent general and then worked his way up steadily through a series of local government and Party posts that took him to the fast-growing eastern provinces of Fujian and Zhejiang, and then briefly to Shanghai. His father was said to have disapproved of the military crackdown on protests in 1989; there is no record of Xi himself ever having stepped away from the Party line.

By 2007, when the five-yearly Party Congress met to choose members of the Politburo and its top body, the Standing Committee, Xi had become the favoured future leadership candidate of the still powerful former leader Jiang Zemin at the head of the 'Shanghai Faction', which had dominated the leadership at the turn of the century. In his mid-fifties, Xi had good contacts with the army and Party establishment, and had built up networks of support in the provinces as well as among officials in Beijing, while steering clear of enmities within the governing hierarchy. He kept his ambitions well disguised and appeared as a safe pair of hands who could be expected not to rock the boat or threaten vested interests in the Party State.

The bureaucratic Hu Jintao, who had been earmarked for the top by Deng in the late 1980s, had not been an impressive leader. He lacked either political clout or charisma and presided over a factionalized Politburo, while Jiang continued to wield influence with strategically placed associates. Hu's weakness brought to fruition Deng's championing of consensus leadership to prevent the emergence of another unconstrained Mao-style figure at the top. He also continued a process of separating the

Party, which maintained overall charge, and the government, which dealt with immediate issues – notably running the economy. This had been the pattern under Jiang when the forceful premier Zhu Rongji was responsible for the fight against inflation, the closing of outdated heavy industry and the preparations for China's entry into the World Trade Organization. Under Hu, Prime Minister Wen Jiabao played the same role and the General Secretary kept out of the direct handling of the economy.

As the 2007 Congress approached, the main question was whether Hu would be able to choose his successor at the end of his second five-year term in 2012. If he advanced his dauphin, Li Keqiang, from his power base in the Party Youth League, he would be founding a political dynasty that would threaten the position of the Jiang faction. Promoting Xi ahead of Li was the obvious way of preventing this.

Jiang got an agreement that all former Politburo Standing Committee members would have to approve of the new line-up at the 2007 Congress. Hu could not muster a majority among this sometimes geriatric group. So, when the members of the Standing Committee filed out of the closed Congress in order of votes received from delegates,

Xi was one place ahead of Li. This meant that, unless something went badly wrong, he would be the next Party boss when Hu and other members of the fourth generation of PRC leaders stepped down on age grounds five years later.

That duly came to pass at the 2012 Congress, with Li getting second place in the Standing Committee and becoming Prime Minister at the annual plenary session of the legislature three months later. Xi also became chair of the Central Military Committee, a highly important post given the PLA's size and political role. The following spring, he also took on the state presidency.

If Jiang and other old-timers thought Xi would show his gratitude and be in their debt, they were in for a shock. If Hu imagined that his acceptance of Xi's rise would create a team of virtual equals with Li, he was equally mistaken. Other princelings discovered that the grouping did not denote mutual loyalty. The most prominent of them, the maverick Bo Xilai, was swiftly brought down in the first of the dramatic trials of 'tigers' who were accused of corruption but were really guilty of presenting a threat to the new leader.

Moving with speed, determination and supreme self-confidence, Xi progressed steadily through five phases of asserting his authority. These inevitably overlap in a system of many layers, but they show the many planes on which he operates as Chairman and Chief Executive Officer of China Inc., its chief financial officer, chief strategist, chief security officer and 'thought leader' – while relegating Li Keqiang to Chief Operating Officer. The process reached its apogee when a Party Plenum in October 2016 declared Xi to be the 'core leader' of the regime.

1 Strengthening the Party and his personal position. In the first year, Xi focused on building up his position and attempting to strengthen the Party by eradicating its weaknesses, especially through the anti-corruption campaign, which its main enforcer, Standing Committee member Wang Qishan, said would be endless. Ensuring a basis of stability for the regime was Xi's prerequisite, with the attendant risk aversion already noted, giving an impression that the leader relishes power for power's sake.

The separation of the Party and the government encouraged by Deng was reversed, with the primacy of the former strengthened. The spreading of authority was checked in favour of centralization. The position of the leader became even more important and, with it, loyalty to him; as an economic adviser put it to me in 2015, 'Who is going to say no to Xi?'

The Party Discipline Commission, which enforces

the anti-corruption drive, is symptomatic of how things have evolved under Xi. It operates outside the law and is not subject to the influence of the government or the courts. It can hold people arbitrarily in secret locations without charges, and invariably ends up by recommending their expulsion from the Communist ranks. They are then handed over to the courts for trial and sentencing – the conviction rate so far has been 100 per cent.

The Commission sits squarely in the heritage of the legalistic code of government which stretches back to the First Emperor, Qin Shi Huang, but which is rarely mentioned by those who vaunt China's Confucian heritage. Legalism has arguably been more important in framing the way China's rulers operate than the more benevolent teachings attributed to the sage. It is founded on the use of the law to scare citizens into submission, extolling secrecy and charismatic authority. From Qin, who was reputed to have buried Confucian scholars alive, to Mao Zedong's violent anti-Confucianism, legalism remained at the core of China's governance.

Dissent has been relentlessly repressed under Xi. Controls on dissemination of information have been strengthened; Xi told media organization that they must 'love the Party, protect the Party and serve the Party'. The campaign against human rights lawyers has led to hundreds being detained; some have reported that they have been tortured. A drive was undertaken to streamline the legal system, not with the aim of introducing the independent rule of law but to make the courts more efficient in imposing Beijing's will in line with legalist practice – all judges in China are required to swear an oath of loyalty to the Party.

A stream of ideological instructions called for adherence to Marxism and denounced 'Western values', which were held to threaten the regime and Chinese culture. (The fact that Marxism came from Europe and hardly fits in with Chinese tradition was not mentioned.) In the summer of 2016, the state media administration banned reports promoting 'Western lifestyles' and insisted that websites use only official news.[2] People invoking the constitution on human rights and freedoms were depicted in official media as 'black hands' seeking to undermine the state at the behest of foreigners. The Minister for Civil Affairs denounced the practice of giving middle-class housing estates Western names – Paris Spring, Roman Holiday, American Gardens or Thames Town – as damaging national sovereignty and dignity.[3] Universities were told what not to teach, with democracy and freedom of speech figuring among proscribed subjects.

Xi's daughter, who had been studying at Harvard, returned home.

The Discipline Commission spread its tentacles through the Party and state system, picking off individuals and networks of influence at national and provincial levels as it attacked the 'cabals' which stood in the leadership's way. Like Bo Xilai, the powerful former boss of the internal security machine, Zhou Yongkang, was given a life sentence for corruption and his family and associates were punished too.

Xi established a coterie of trusted advisers, including natives of Shaanxi Province, where his father was born and where Xi himself went during his years as a 'sent-down youth' in the Cultural Revolution. He drew on loyal lieutenants from his early adult years and from his time in the eastern provinces. Through the process of 'Party strengthening', accompanied by a rolling series of ideological dictates, Xi sought to solidify his personification of the monopoly political movement's ideology, emotions and virtues as the leader who would realize the 'China Dream'.[4]

2 Tightening control of the armed forces, domestic security and the law. During his second year in power, Xi tightened his grip on the armed forces (the PLA) and the internal security apparatus, including the million-strong People's Armed Police, and exerted greater control over the legal system. The army was hit by an anti-corruption drive against profiteering generals; this was accompanied by a shake-up of the command structure to centralize authority – together with plans to modernize the forces by concentrating on the navy and missile units and reducing the size of the two-million-strong standing army. Xi's assumption of the Chair of the Central Military Commission in 2012 had been in line with his predecessors, though he took the job more quickly than Hu had done. But then, in 2016, he added the post of commander-in-chief, which not even Mao had held. Just as the government had been brought firmly under the control of the Party, so the central political machine asserts, in Xi's person, its grip on the armed forces. The PLA newspaper was moved to hail the leader's vision as 'like seeing a ship's mast in the sea, like seeing the radiant sun rise in the east ... the cosmic truth'.[5]

Control of domestic policing and legal affairs was assured by the defenestration of Zhou Yongkang, whose influence permeated the oil and gas industry and the most heavily populated province of Sichuan as well as the police and legal system. Xi took over direct control of the internal security apparatus. Trusted lieutenants were installed in key positions and conducted purges of real or imagined adversaries who might threaten the General Secretary's authority, using extra-legal methods as they wanted.

3 Raising the global profile. In 2015 alone, Xi made 14 state visits abroad as he took a highly active role in raising China's international profile in pursuit of the goal of achieving equality with the United States. He put his personal stamp on the 'One Belt, One Road' programme of aid and infrastructure projects stretching across Asia and into Europe; if the plan was to be implemented in full, expenditure would be likely to run into trillions of dollars. The PRC launched the $100 billion Asian Infrastructure Investment Bank to rival the Asian Development Bank backed by Japan and the United States; despite opposition from Washington, it attracted more than 50 other countries, including leading European nations, and marked a definite diplomatic success for Beijing. China offered financial assistance to countries from Britain to Ecuador, bolstered the relationship with Russia and promoted a scheme for an Asian free trade zone as an alternative to the Trans-Pacific Partnership of a dozen nations pushed by Washington.

At the same time, Xi's administration pressed ahead with its building of bases on reclaimed reefs in the South China Sea to back up its sovereignty claims there, taking no notice of the disapproval of neighbours and the UN tribunal that ruled against it in the summer of 2016. It also maintained a tough posture towards Japan and limited its role in bringing sanctions to bear on North Korea for fear of provoking regime collapse in Pyongyang.

4 *Taking charge of the economy.* In the summer of 2015, Xi added the economy to his array of direct interests. The Party Leading Groups on economics and economic reform, which he chairs, took on a more active role in policy formulation, supplanting the government and its technocrats. Tellingly, the US Treasury began to deal directly with the group on economic affairs rather than, as in the past, with a government minister. When Janet Yellen, the Chair of the Federal Reserve, visited Beijing in 2016, the person she wanted to see apart from Zhou Xiaochian, the Governor of the Central Bank, was Liu He, the Secretary of the Leading Group.

In keeping with the imposition of discipline Party-style, economists were given a line to follow. The flow of information was restricted. An increasing number of disillusioned bureaucrats sought employment in the private sector. A group of economists published an open letter with official approval, urging that university economics courses should be more Marxist and saying that students should not be 'brainwashed by Western theories'. 'The Westernization of economics was one of the reasons for the collapse of the Soviet Union,' the letter added.[6]

The results were far from impressive. An attempt to foster a stronger stock exchange turned sour and undermined the policy of encouraging companies to seek equity financing rather than building up more bank debts. A crucial reform of the way in which the currency's value was fixed was mishandled. Official statements on state enterprises boiled down to a call for greater Communist Party control and a signal lack of proposals to increase competition. A campaign to promote supply-side economics lacked substance.

There was an admission in an anonymous article run prominently in the principal Party newspaper in the summer of 2016 that things were not going to plan, but this was immediately followed by publication of a more reassuring 'blue skies' speech by Xi. These developments gave a strong impression that the Party elite had taken up the reins of economic management but did not know how to manage the delicate balance between state control and reform. After all, a leader like Xi who has lived all his life in the cocoon of the Communist system may not have an appreciation of how economic reform with market characteristics works – and may hope to strengthen the system rather than change it in fundamental ways that will, inevitably, contain dangers to the Party State, whose strengthening is his prime concern.[7]

5 Preparing for the Congress. With that strengthening in mind, beginning in 2016, Xi focused on domestic campaigns to reinforce his position and that of the Party, with which he identified himself. A hundred thousand young people were recruited to support the official line on websites, their job defined as being to 'resolutely and totally engage in a life-or-death struggle with harmful content and those who propagate it'.[8] The leader still made foreign trips, but his prime concern was the long run-up to the Party Congress at the end of 2017.

The Discipline Commission continued its wide-ranging activities with regulations to punish Party members who did not carry out central policies adequately. This was part of Xi's efforts to promote officials who understood the policies he backed and could implement them. He used the anti-corruption campaign to attack associates of Hu Jintao, including the purging of Ling Jihua, who had been Chief of Staff to his predecessor. The Youth League came under investigation by the Commission. So did the Party Propaganda Department, where Jiang associates remained influential. Other figures connected with Jiang were ousted by the anti-graft drive in both the armed forces and provincial administrations.

Xi's underlying aim was to keep the former chieftains from influencing the choice of the Politburo and its Standing Committee at the Congress. Five of the seven members of the Committee were due to step down on age grounds and Xi needed to be able to choose their successors to be sure of a loyal and efficient team for his second five-year term and beyond.

As he made his preparations, Xi and China faced some fundamental political issues which had been latent when he took over at the end of 2012 but which emerged with growing force in his early years at the summit of the system set in place by Mao nearly seven decades earlier. To take the principal ones:

• How can China be a Communist state when its Prime Minister declares that 'we will make an all-round effort to deepen market-oriented reform' and when private enterprise played such a key role in driving growth in the years after Deng's initial reforms? One answer is that the Communist Party should be seen as an instrument of power and not as an ideological movement, despite the profiles of Marx, Engels and Lenin emblazoned on the walls of official buildings. Ideology had come to play a lesser role under Deng, Jiang and Hu but Xi has revived it. This may be more in the way of setting a line for the Chinese to toe than a belief in the ideology, which, under a strict reading of the anti-Western dictates of recent years, should be beyond the pale. As Xi's record since 2012 has shown, what matters above all for him is centralized authority. A strong Communist Party (whatever its name and professed beliefs) is the best means to achieve that in a Leninist system where it enjoys supremacy over the government and is held to be infallible,

• Then one might ask how the leaders pay obeisance to the notion of Communist equality in a country with well over 100 known dollar billionaires, many of whom sit in the annual plenary sessions of the two houses of the national legislature. But, as Deng is reported to have said (though there is no record of him actually uttering the words), it is glorious to get rich. Despite the anti-corruption drive and the disapproval of conspicuous consumption under Xi, consumerism remains the most powerful driver for the citizens of the PRC, as shown by the relative failure of earlier attempts to reduce inequalities.

- Where does the Party's legitimacy lie? Improving the standard of living has undoubtedly been central to any answer to this question, as has the relatively stability since the crackdown of 1989. The bargain which the regime made then with its citizens, that it would provide the framework for rising wealth so long as they did not concern themselves with politics or offer organized dissent to the ruling caste, has held. But the denial of a political role to the mass of the population is a negative foundation for government. Seeking stability for stability's sake is a limited objective, even if, given China's past, it has considerable force.

Xi attributes the collapse of the Soviet Union to a loss of belief in Communism. 'The negation of Lenin and Stalin ... spawned historical nihilism and the confusion of thoughts.' Cleaving to Marxism is vital, he adds. Mao Zedong Thought is the foundation of the regime, and it is a grave mistake, Xi argues, to draw a distinction between the Great Helmsman's era and the subsequent time of reform and opening up. Rather, the PRC's history must be seen as a continuum in which the Party never made mistakes. However wrong, the script has its inner logic as it seeks to serve his basic aim of strengthening the Party.[9]

In his stress on Marxist-Maoism, Xi appears to be seeking something more than material improvement as a basis for rule. But it has not been very convincing, particularly for younger urban residents, for whom ideology means little and whose way of life escapes the confines of the Party system. The one-child policy may have been somewhat relaxed in 2015, but the state still reserves the right to interfere in such an intensely personal field. Moreover, although China is in many ways a far freer place for its citizens than at any time since 1949, and material progress and modernity have brought considerable individual liberation, the security apparatus remains very powerful and has been steadily strengthened in recent years, with police often exercising arbitrary authority.

Legal liberalization has stopped and the leaders have made it clear that the role of the law is to strengthen the Party: when a new President of the

Supreme People's Court took office in 2013, he praised his predecessor for having maintained 'a firm political stand'. The Nobel Peace Prize winner of 2010, Liu Xiaobo, is, as noted earlier, in prison for 11 years for having circulated a petition calling for democracy, and his brother-in-law was sent to jail for 11 years, too, for fraud in 2013, a case widely seen as an example of official retribution against the dissident's family.

People who travel from the provinces to present petitions in Beijing may be held in clandestine 'black jails' or incarcerated in psychiatric wards. The blind lawyer Chen Guangcheng, who campaigned against abuses of the one-child policy, including forced abortions, was put under house arrest, then jailed, then returned to house arrest and beaten before escaping to the United States in 2012. A group of women who petitioned against forced abortion under the one-child policy told *Le Monde* in 2013 of one camp in north-east China where they were subjected to torture and forced to work for up to 15 hours a day, being paid 5 to 25 yuan (82 cents to $4.10) a month for making jackets for companies in Australia and Italy, shirts for South Korea and trousers for the PLA.[10]

The recurrent warnings about nefarious foreign activity give the impression of a regime that is more worried than it needs to be about its position. The orders banning reports that promote Western entertainment raise questions about just how far the leadership sees itself as the nation's moral guardian and whether it wants to ban such staples of modern life as pop music, Hollywood films or television programmes accessed through the Internet.

This attachment to ideological ballast has its roots in the heritage of the imperial centuries. The central power believes it is the fount of all wisdom, and that if this is questioned the whole semi-divine system risks crashing to earth, as shown by Mikhail Gorbachev's experiment with liberalization in the USSR. This fits with the Chinese tradition, which has little or no place for incremental adaptation. The country has never known a peaceful regime change; it is a matter of all or nothing: revolts, civil wars, invasions, violence – far from what admirers praise as China's innate virtues of reason.

After six decades of Communist rule, it is perfectly true that the nature of the system in the PRC makes change extremely difficult. The Party dominates like no political movement in the West. That may be a source of admiration for some observers, but brings with it systemic weakness which grows in scope as China develops, and is the biggest bar to the PRC dominating the world.

The seven-man – all its members are male – Standing Committee of the Party's Political Bureau (Politburo) sits at the apex of power. Around it are the wider, 25-person Politburo – currently including two women – and the Party Central Committee with 200 full members and 170 non-voting alternates. The Prime Minister belongs to the Standing Committee – the current incumbent ranks second to Xi Jinping.

There are Communist cells in every state agency, from the central bank to local planning authorities, and in all companies of any size. Visiting the headquarters of the big search engine Baidu in 2013, Zhao Leji, head of the Organization Department of the Party's Central Committee, said corporate cultures should be 'consistent with socialist core values'. Documents on reform of SOEs issued in 2015–16 stated that greater Party control was the path to better performance. 'Major operational management arrangements ... must be studied and discussed by the Party committees before any decision by the board of directors or company management,' the main Communist ideological periodical, *Qiushi*, decreed in mid-2016.[11]

The Party is present in sports organizations, charities and entertainment troupes. As a professor told the author Richard McGregor, it is like God:

everywhere but you just can't see it. The regime's main newspaper, the *People's Daily*, compares the 'sacred Party spirit' to 'a Christian's belief in God'.[12] The Party's achievement in 'leading the Chinese people to build a new China is no less than Moses leading the Israelites out of Egypt', it added.[13]

To start to dismantle or reorientate this enormous apparatus would be a daunting task in itself. Many of those who would have to accept change have a strong interest in maintaining the status quo. This is not simply a matter of politicians retaining power, given the Party's extensive reach and the power elite it has bred. State enterprises are integral to the system and their bosses have considerable political clout as they move between business and government in the PRC's nomenklatura. Relatives of powerful figures enjoy promotion and wealth. Even private companies often depend on their links with the Party and state, their senior executives sitting in the central or provincial legislatures. Politicians everywhere covet power, of course, as do their parties and their business connections.

What marks China is the way in which the elite sees itself as having an unquestionable grip on authority, allowing no opposition or prospect of change. If stability is regarded as a high priority, it is stability on Communist Party terms. That is not the case in Western democracies, where the regime and the administration or government are separate and where there is debate and dialogue, however flawed and influenced by money, sectarianism or prejudice. The democratic system enables peaceful change; indeed, in some democracies, frequent change has become an integral part of the process, sometimes with disruptive effects. In the PRC, no alternative is allowed to emerge. The need to show the wisdom and unity of the Party is held to be paramount, whatever differences may exist behind the scenes. There can be no mercy for those who do not submit to its rule.

The combination of these factors prevents China going through a process of political evolution to match the growth of the economy and the changes in society. This is underpinned by a further issue, which can be summarized as follows: why should China change? Has it not achieved so much for its citizens under Communist rule that it would be folly to alter course? As Xi says repeatedly, the PRC must be true to its past, both Maoist and Dengist. The danger of this is that adherence to tradition becomes stultifying, strengthening the vested interests built up over more than 60 years and preventing the change China needs.

The longer this immobility persists, the more

difficult reform is rendered through the accretion of power by the status quo and the attractions of continuing as before. Deng could push through his economic revolution because the old ways had lost credibility and there was a hunger for experimentation of a different kind from Mao's adventurism – indeed there was a hunger to get away from the traumas of the previous decades and to introduce a human element into the story of Communist China. Now, in contrast, Xi proclaims the importance of recognizing the contribution of the first three decades of Communist rule to the country's renaissance and warns against experimentation that does not accord with that past.

The next two chapters will analyse the growing challenges facing China economically and socially. But in the system installed since 1949, it is the politics that count most, and they come with a heavy historical inheritance coloured by the extraordinary ups and downs experienced by many of the top leaders of the People's Republic, from Mao and his colleagues through to the 'sent-down' Xi Jinping. As we have seen, the launch of economic reform and opening up by Deng Xiaoping was, at base, a political calculation aimed at preserving one-party rule. The brutal suppression of the 1989 protests centred on Tiananmen Square in Beijing (though the repression stretched far beyond the square and to other cities across the PRC) was only the most naked instance of the use of violence to preserve the system. Though Deng relaunched economic reform through market mechanisms in 1992 after a temporary withdrawal and a brief conservative hiatus, his basic purpose was always clear and his ruthlessness was never in doubt.

Deng's belief in Communism was no doubt genuine, though he was primarily a practical operator, crossing the river by feeling the stones underfoot. But his career before the Tiananmen massacre, including the suppression of the Democracy Wall dissidents in 1979 and the jailing for 15 years of their leading figure, Wei Jingsheng, showed him, above all, as a believer in force to assert political power.

Once that force had been asserted, there was no reason to question why it had been required. This is a regime whose self-protectiveness borders on paranoia bred by decades of fighting for survival followed by the traumas of Mao's erratic dictatorship and his recurrent purges. Enemies were always there if they needed to be invoked, as in the case of 1989 'black hands' and foreign agents who were held to have exploited the student protests to try to bring down the socialist system and install a bourgeois republic as the vassal of the West. From this it was a straight course to buttressing the existing system with no questions asked. 'What should we do from now on?', the paramount leader asked after the repression of 1989. 'We should continue to follow unswervingly the basic line, principles and policies we have formulated.' A quarter of a century later, Tiananmen Square and the more bloody killing of citizens on the road leading into the centre of the capital remain a taboo subject.

In his remarks to the press after becoming General Secretary at the end of 2012, Xi Jinping defined the Party's role as being to rally the nation 'in taking over the relay baton passed on to us by history, and in making continued efforts to achieve the great renewal of the Chinese nation, make the Chinese nation stand rock-firm in the family of nations, and make even greater contribution to mankind'. But, like a mid-dynasty emperor facing reality, he went on to acknowledge that 'under the new conditions, our Party faces many severe challenges, and there are also many pressing problems within the Party that need to be resolved, particularly corruption, being divorced from the people, going through formalities and bureaucratism caused by some Party officials'.

The Chinese people, he said, 'wish to have better education, more stable jobs, more income, greater social security, better medical and health care, improved housing conditions, and a better environment. They want their children to have sound growth, have good jobs and lead a more enjoyable life.'

Polls showed high levels of public support for this – yet there is an evident lack of faith in the system on top of which the leaders sit. There is a sentiment, akin to that of imperial days, that the far-off rulers in Beijing are benevolent figures who would put right the misdemeanours of local officials if only they knew the truth. Like the grasping, corrupt imperial magistrates, it is the bureaucrats with whom people come into contact in their everyday lives who are seen as the villains. One major question running through this book is whether that verdict will remain in place as people start to ask why the system as a whole cannot provide them with the protection that should be expected from a government.

Much of the loyalty the regime commands comes down to relief that China has escaped from the turbulence of the period from the 1830s to the mid-1970s, during which it went through the worst protracted tribulations of any nation on earth. For the average inhabitant, this is probably the best time to be Chinese. But satisfaction is largely predicated on the delivery of crude material progress, which could now become less of a trump card as growth slows and social tensions rise.

The wealth gap leaves many, many millions resentful; while the poor have become less poor during the era of economic growth, the rich have grown even richer. For the first decade of this century, the government did not publish the Gini coefficient measuring inequality, presumably because of the embarrassment and outrage it would have caused. When it was finally put out at the end of 2011, it was officially recorded at 0.45, with 0 representing absolute equality and 1 absolute inequality. This was below South Africa and Brazil but well ahead of the United States, Britain, India and Japan. A separate report by Chengdu University placed the figure for 2010 at 0.61 and evaluated the combined income of households in the rich eastern provinces as 2.7 times that of the west and the central regions, with 10 per cent of households holding up to 57 per cent of all disposable income.[14]

Then a survey by Peking University reported that, in 2012, the richest 5 per cent earned 23 per cent of China's total household income and those in the lowest 5 per cent earned 0.1 per cent of that income. Average annual income for urban families was 60 per cent higher than in rural areas. Incomes in Shanghai were two-and-half times those in Gansu Province in the north-west ($2,000, £1,200).[15]

In a less concentrated political system, some of the challenges facing China could be dealt with by the institutions of civil society, but in the PRC everything leads to the central organ of control. This is becoming a weakness which will hobble China but which, given the nature of the Party, may be beyond remedy. The basic issue is one of embedded control, which the regime has pursued since 1949, but which is increasingly difficult to enforce in a rapidly evolving society with a myriad of sectional and regional elements and powerful vested interests. The model which took shape under Deng no longer reaps the dividends of the first stage of development but is producing a fast-evolving, increasingly independent-minded society out of kilter with the official mantras and the Party's proclamation of itself as the sole representative of the people of China. The very force and scale of Xi's campaign to enforce the regime's authority may be a measure of the size of the problem he and his colleagues face.

Though so many things have changed, the Party State has not wished – or been able – to adapt its top-down approach to power. Western-style democracy is not an option: the essential underpinnings are absent, not least the rule of law.

Moreover, admirers of China's system made much of the rise of Donald Trump in 2016 as a warning sign of what the American system could bring, even though some surveys showed considerable admiration for the Republican candidate's style among the Chinese.

Yet the core equation is coming to the end of its useful life, not only economically but also politically. The system implemented by Mao, continued by Deng and taken up by their successors is increasingly in conflict with the way China is evolving. To maintain the momentum essential for the system requires change. As Prime Minister Wen Jiabao put it, 'Without the success of political structural reforms, economic structural reforms cannot be carried out in full, and whatever gains we have made may be lost.'

However, the ability to think out of the Mao–Deng box has become ever more limited after a decade of inertia under Hu and Wen. Xi's insistence that the PRC's history is a continuum and that the greatest priority is the preservation of Party power brings with it the danger that maintaining the status quo will be rated more important than the necessary maturing of the nation, holding back its evolution in the straitjacket imposed by the ruling political movement.

3

The Middle Development Trap

It was in 2007 that Wen Jiabao unveiled his 'four uns'. China's economy, he said as he ended his first five years as Prime Minister, was unsustainable, uncoordinated, unbalanced and unstable. This may have seemed strange to those who regard China's trajectory as one of virtually unalloyed progress, but the Premier repeated the warning in terms which left no doubt about his awareness of the problems facing what appeared to be the world's most successful major economy. However, nothing happened as the Party establishment weighed in to block reform, and the reaction of Wen's own government to the downturn at the end of 2008 produced a short-term recovery but with a negative longer-term impact. As he and Hu Jintao stepped down in 2012–13, their 10 years in office looked like a lost decade when it came to adapting the

PRC to the more testing environment in the second decade of the 21st century.

Wen's successor, Li Keqiang, who has a doctorate in economics, gave his approval to a report by a group set up by the State Council and the World Bank which called for the PRC to 'complete its transition to a market economy – through enterprise, land, labour, and financial sector reforms – strengthen its private sector, open its markets to greater competition and innovation, and ensure equality of opportunity to help achieve its goal of a new structure for economic growth'. It proposed to dismantle the state monopolies in key sectors and to raise productivity.[1]

After becoming Prime Minister in March 2013, Li made statements pledging 'an all-round effort to deepen market-oriented reform, unleash the dividends of change, and continue to grow the economy, improving livelihoods and promoting social equity'. He spoke of carrying out a 'self-imposed revolution' in the economy. 'All of society is ardently awaiting new breakthroughs in reform,' a government directive declared. Li even spoke of potential pain as China went into cold turkey to shed its high-growth habit.[2]

Given China's economic achievements, the question might be asked: what needs to be changed after such a successful record? For an answer, turn to Wen's 'four uns'.

(1) The economy was unsustainable. Industrialization since the 1980s had neglected fundamental long-term issues in favour of short-term results – in sharp contrast to the image of the PRC as the home of efficient, long-term planning. The system implemented by the ruling caste had promoted many of these fault lines, including the enormous environmental crisis, which will be described in the next chapter. In contrast to the picture of China bestriding the world economically, the country remained dependent on raw materials from abroad.

Water was in short supply in northern China – indeed, Wen Jiabao warned in 1999 that the shortage threatened the survival of the nation.[3] But the low controlled price levels encourage wastage. Little had been done to check the potential disastrous shortfall in northern wheat-growing regions as urban demand rocketed owing to the expansion of Beijing, Tianjin and other big cities. Desalination was at an early stage and its costs were higher than the average selling price. The south–north water diversion project begun in 2002 was planned to pump 45 billion cubic metres a year from the Yangtze and its tributaries, but it was not due for completion until the middle of this century and there was no telling the impact on the level or quality of rivers and their eco-systems. There was a vicious circle between two resources of which China is short, water and energy; development of shale gas and nuclear power to help meet energy demand was constrained by a shortage of the water needed in both processes, while desalination used a lot of energy, on which China is trying to economize.

Urbanization had boosted the proportion of city residents from 18 to 53 per cent of the population since 1980 and was expected to reach 70 per cent by 2030 with an annual influx of 15–20 million from the countryside. But it had been pursued with scant attention to developing sustainable, liveable cities, and the numbers mean more than two hundred centres with more than a million residents by 2030, with all the attendant strains this will bring.

(2) The economy was uncoordinated. Growth had come from exports and fixed asset investment in construction and infrastructure. Consumption played a much smaller role and had fallen as a proportion of GDP this century – overall consumption accounted for just 50 per cent of GDP and household consumption for only 35 per cent, far below the global average. The services sector fell behind (from an already low base) as manufacturing boomed.

The Middle Development Trap

Capital took the lion's share of economic expansion while wages represented a far lower slice of national income. With low interest rates, households got small returns on their savings, which were channelled to fund projects in what is known as financial repression – taking the money of the people to fund the state and its elite of government bodies, companies and individuals.

The result was an unhealthy reliance on more and more construction to keep up the GDP figures, with major misallocation of capital and a declining rate of return on projects approved by officials whose promotion prospects were boosted by delivering crude growth numbers. At the same time, the fact that most tax revenue went to the central government meant local authorities were short of cash to meet spending obligations; to fill the gap, they requisitioned farm land, classified it for development and sold it to developers, with social consequences we will see in the next chapter. Or they borrowed, increasing the debt burden.

The Five-Year Plan for 2011–15 provided for rebalancing from investment and exports to consumption and services. Sales abroad did, indeed, fall, with the trade surplus component of GDP dropping from 10 per cent in 2007 to 2.6 per cent in 2012 as the world economy slowed after the financial crisis. But investment rose as a share of GDP in 2012, while that of household consumption declined. Services edged up by only 1.4 per cent between 2010 and 2012. The reason was simple: for all Wen Jiabao's fine talk of the need to shift the economy, his bigger concern was to maintain growth, which meant falling back on the short-term recipe of pumping more cash into infrastructure projects and maintaining property construction.

(3) The economy was unbalanced. Alongside the mismatch between investment and consumption, development had been largely concentrated in coastal areas following the initial 'Special Economic Zones' (SEZs) set up under Deng to spearhead growth. Inland China fell behind, especially the countryside, which constitutes most of the country's landmass. The report by Chengdu University mentioned earlier found that, in 2010, the combined income of households in eastern provinces was 2.7 times that of the west and the central regions. Deprived of rights in the places where they worked, migrant workers form an underclass of more than 150 million.

While China is indeed set to overtake the United States in absolute GDP size, it will lag far behind for decades in per capita terms, though, of course, a dollar or its equivalent in yuan buys far more in the PRC than it does in the United States. Rankings by the IMF and other international bodies in the second decade of this century put China anywhere from 86th to 114th in wealth per inhabitant, with more than 100 million people below the $1.25-a-day international poverty line. As the World Bank wrote in a report in 2012: 'With the second largest number of poor in the world after India, poverty reduction remains a fundamental challenge' for the PRC. The IMF, meanwhile, noted: 'High income inequality and environmental problems are further signs that the current growth model needs to change,' saying in mid-2013 that such a shift was 'increasingly urgent'.[4]

(4) The economy was unstable. These inequalities have led to discontent, augmented by an array of social factors that will be dealt with in the next chapter. But apart from 150,000 to 180,000 protests each year, the elements listed above produce an unstable economic structure which stands in sharp contrast to the progress shown in the top-line data of the past decades, as exemplified by the reaction to the 2008 downturn analysed in Chapter 1.

The tightening that was needed to contain that huge credit and spending bubble slowed the official figure for growth to 9.2 per cent in 2011, 7.8 per cent in 2012 and 7.5 per cent in mid-2013. Lending switched from state banks to 'shadow banking': raising money through trust companies, wealth management products and corporate bonds. As a result, the overall debt burden as a proportion of GDP in China rose by 84 per cent between 2008 and 2013, twice as much as it had done in the United States in the five years before the 2008 crisis.[5]

That switchback pattern revealed a fifth 'un': China's economy was uncontrolled. As he stepped down in 2001 after bringing down inflation, streamlining the state sector and ushering China into the World Trade Organization, Prime Minister Zhu Rongji proposed a target of annual growth of 7 per cent for the following five years; the actual average was 10.4 in 2003–6.

The target for the Five-Year Plan for 2006–10 was 7.5 per cent for the whole period, with 8 per cent for 2007; but the final figure for that year was 13 per cent. The Five-Year Plan for 2011–15 provided for 7 per cent annual expansion in pursuit of a more sustainable economic course and rebalancing away from dependence on fixed-asset investments in the shape of infrastructure and construction towards increased consumption as a driver of the economy. The number for 2011 was 9.2 per cent and, despite a significant subsequent slowdown, 2012 was still almost one point ahead of projections at 7.8 per cent.

Such numbers may have delighted China bulls when compared to anaemic data from developed economies, European ones in particular – though even they have started to recognize the dangers of runaway expansion. But the variance between the forecasts and the numbers finally announced cast doubts on the accuracy of China's planners or their prowess as policy enforcers. Their schemes are often slow to mature. The device used to take the bad loans of the big four banks off their balance sheets before they issued shares at the turn of the century is a good example of how slow progress often is: 15 years later, 60 per cent of the money advanced by the state to fund this operation remained outstanding and the recovery rate on the loans was 20 per cent.

The constant rolling out of plans may appear impressive to those who dismiss the short-termism of democratic governments that have to win elections but they are, all too often, not carried out as laid down on paper, while basic questions remain over the validity of the underlying data. In part, this is because of the sheer difficulty of administering a country as large as China with a limited corps of civil servants and the age-old tension between the centre and the provinces. Tellingly, Li Keqiang, whose reservations about the figures have already been noted, felt he had to spell out in one of his early speeches as Premier that 'the central government will lead by example. Local governments must follow suit.'[6]

This flaw in what is meant to be a smooth, top-down system is greatly exacerbated by the structural weaknesses in the economy, which contribute powerfully to the 'four uns'. Headlong growth masked these weaknesses when the 'China model' seemed all-triumphant; now they have to be addressed if the PRC is to continue to move forward. But in each case there are powerful political and systemic forces working against the change which the leaders know is required, but from which they have shrunk for fear of weakening the regime.

Starting at the base, agriculture needs a thorough shake-up. All farmland belongs to the state. It is distributed to rural households on a leasehold basis – extended from 30 to 60 years in 2009 in a compromise at the end of an internal debate about whether to grant ownership rights to farmers. That was refused for three reasons: a remaining ideological argument in favour of state possession; the desire of local authorities to retain the right to requisition land to raise money; and the fear on the part of city authorities of an influx of people from the countryside who would have sold their land and moved to urban areas which could not absorb them.

The leasehold system means that Chinese farming is characterized by small plots which can support a family but do not permit more efficient, mechanized operations. The flood of migrant workers from rural areas to cities produces a shortage of people of working age who know how to farm. Education in anything but basic agricultural technology is sparse. Moreover, pollution, often carried by rivers, damages farmland, while poor-quality nitrate fertilizers leach out the soil and toxic chemical waste infects crops, including rice.

Urbanization, pollution and desertification are eating into arable land – China is at the lower limit of the acreage it needs to feed itself under the government's policy of 95 per cent self-sufficiency (except for soy). The water shortage adds to the pressure in the wheat-growing regions of the north, where the aquifers are drying up and available supplies are diverted to mega-cities. The logistics of food distribution are poorly developed, with a lack of refrigerated transport and warehouses. There are some big producers of China's favourite meat, pork, but many of the animals are kept by small farmers who breed and slaughter a few pigs according to short-term market movements, producing alternate gluts and shortages that fuel inflation as the cycle turns.

As for China's vast army of migrant workers, the *hukou* household registration system means they have qualified for health, education, welfare, pension and property rights only in their homeplace; some relaxation of the system is being introduced but will only come into effect over a ten-year period or longer. This has important social repercussions, as will be laid out in the next chapter. It also constricts the labour market. As the government encourages the development of the inland areas from which most of the migrants come, companies in the coastal regions have to increase wages to attract them, boosting costs at a time when China faces growing competition from other developing nations.

Local government finance is in a parlous state in many parts of the country, pushing provincial and sub-provincial authorities to depend on sales of land and loans to meet spending obligations. The financial sector, under the control of the state and its big banks, has been the scene of major misallocation of capital as loan policy was decided by administrative quotas, with cash going overwhelmingly to state enterprises. Financial repression of households encouraged them to go after the far greater wealth enhancement offered by property.

Since private ownership of real estate was introduced at the end of the 1990s, the economy has become uncomfortably reliant on the continuing health of the residential market, with nearly 90 per cent of families fully or partially owning their homes and surveys showing more than 10 per cent having two or more homes. The volatility of the 70 or so different urban property markets across the country is a constant source of concern, for instance, as prices are stable in second- and third-tier cities but soared by 50 per cent in a few months in 2016 in the boom city of Shenzhen in the south. The authorities have to spend too much time fine-tuning these different markets with adjustments to mortgage rates and other regulations to ensure that young people can get on the property ladder while their middle-class elders who have invested in second and third holdings are not alienated by a slowdown in values.[7]

Cheap credit from the big banks cushions inefficient state enterprises. But the rising level of debt increases pressure on the financial system, and government attempts to spread that risk have produced an array of financial instruments on offer from agents, ranging from wealth management companies to outright Ponzi schemes, some of which went spectacularly bust in 2015–16.

The lack of an independent legal system, weak accountability and regulation, plus the legacy of deep-rooted corruption, mean that business is conducted on a potentially shifting basis in which the fall of a political protector can bring down a company, decision-making is opaque and dodges proliferate.

Services have grown significantly, particularly those linked to ecommerce and mobile telephones in big cities and to travel and entertainment. Professional services are also set to increase. But the rate of expansion of retail consumption has been soggy. Together, these have not been sufficient to offset the negative impact of the decline in heavy industry exacerbated by excess capacity in sectors such as steel, glass, aluminium and oil refining, which has brought deflation in its wake. By 2016, five provinces were in or close to recession – the three regions of the old industrial north-east, the coal centre of Shanxi and the steel-making province of Hebei, around Beijing. Some other areas were still doing well, such as Chongqing in the south-west, but the scale of the industrial renovation required was far greater than the government's limited response. Short-term stimulus programmes and monetary easing produced a series of mini-cycles within the overall descending growth corridor. This pattern militated against bold reforms that would have led to more downward pressure at a time when the administration wanted to put a floor under the decline and prepare for the Party Congress in 2017.

On top of this, though corporate expansion continued, some overseas forays were turning sour. Investments in natural resources overseas were hit by the fall in world commodity prices, spurred largely by the slowdown in the PRC. Big property developers pulled back from projects in Europe and Australia, while ambitious conglomerates and insurance firms abandoned acquisition plans.

The drive to integrate the PRC's financial markets with the rest of the world has been bumpy and casts a further shadow over the vision of China being run by meritocratic experts who invariably know what they are doing. Instead, the mainland has experienced a series of bubbles – in property, in the stock market, in bonds and in more exotic sectors such as jade, fine tea and medicinal plants.

The government bid in 2015 to pump up the Shanghai stock market to encourage companies to issue shares to raise funding rather than going for yet more bank loans ran into trouble. The bubble set off largely by official encouragement predictably burst.

Rather than let prices find their natural level, the authorities ordered state financial groups dubbed 'the national team' to intervene to the tune of several hundred billion dollars. That checked the fall but destroyed the notion of market value. By the late summer of 2016, the Shanghai A share index was 40 per cent below the peak, though support measures meant it was still trading at a 35 per cent premium to the better-regulated Hong Kong index.

In the summer of 2016, for the second year running, the international MSCI index decided not to include mainland China in its global basket of shares – only stocks traded in Hong Kong or the United States were covered. One major reason was that investors who put money into mainland shares were limited in their ability to get their cash out if they decide to sell. The same applies to the PRC government bond market: it is among the largest in the world, but foreigners have been naturally cautious about finding their investments trapped behind a great wall of regulation. Having unveiled the prospect of speedy reform to bring their markets into line with international practice, the authorities provoked disappointment among big international investors by the slow pace of action in practice.

They provided further cause for concern about their ability to deal with markets when they mishandled a change in the way the value of the currency was fixed in August 2015, setting off flurries in international markets which persisted through 2016. After those experiences, the reform-minded governor of the central bank remarked in an interview that change was still on the agenda but only when it was 'convenient'. Sources in Beijing made it clear that technocrats like him had been forced to give way to the politicians as the Party took over the commanding heights of the economy, with less than happy results.

There were collateral effects. Taking heed of the likelihood of the currency depreciating, Chinese companies shifted into dollars, increasing monetary outflows and causing speculation that the central bank and those who gave it instructions might have lost control. Calm returned, but only at the cost of intervention totalling almost $500 billion. Worries about the Chinese currency and stocks persisted as it became clear that talk of market-led reform and internationalization of the renminbi had not shaken the authorities' fundamental taste for control and manipulation.

The pressure on lenders crowded out private companies, which were the main motors of growth and job creation; one state bank manager told the author in mid-2016 that policy had changed to focus on state enterprises. Private investment faltered as a result as companies concentrated on their core activities rather than seeking to expand.

The ultimate danger of such policy uncertainty and mishandling is that domestic households, whose savings are the bedrock of the economy, could lose confidence and shift their assets abroad, despite the barriers to doing so. As a result, the full liberalization of the currency, one of the ultimate goals of economic reform, seems far off. Control and liberalizing reform make uneasy bed-fellows – but that is what China's system has stuck itself with.

The Deng economic revolution remains only half accomplished. The second part is likely to be considerably more testing than the first, with the evaporation of the equation between cheap labour and cheap capital and the decline in world trade evident in 2015–16.

Like motherhood and apple pie, reform is generally regarded as being automatically a good thing. There was an assumption at the end of 2012 that the advent of new men to run China must mean new policies which would usher in a new era. We have seen how little evidence there is for this in the political sphere, with a spill-over into economic policy-making. The power of the Party's interests, and its ability to defend them, constitute a major brake on progress, especially in the state sector, where loss-making companies are protected because they guarantee jobs and provide local activity.

To take one example the author came across in 2015. A sizeable steel company decided to close down a mill outside a provincial capital. The local Communist Party Secretary vetoed this on the grounds that 5,000 jobs were involved, the province drew tax revenue from the plant and he 'wanted a steel mill in his city'. The company went to the government in Beijing and got approval for the closure plan. The Secretary went to the central Party apparatus and had the decision countermanded. The mill went on operating, at a loss.

Structural reform would reduce growth and increase inflation for several years while provoking unemployment, which an administration fixated on the need for stability wants to avoid. Here the role of the state-owned enterprises is key.

The SOEs, which are mainstays of the Party State, ride on subsidies and preferential treatment. Though they contribute only 22 per cent of economic output, they account for 55 per cent of corporate debt and are, in the words of the IMF, 'essentially on life support'.[8] If reform affected this through increased input prices for energy and water and greater cost of capital, many SOEs would go into loss. Their position would be even more perilous if they were shorn of their monopolies and oligopolies, and faced competition from private or foreign companies. Their profits have fallen steadily. Half the SOEs under the umbrella of the central administration, known as SASAC, made a loss in 2015. State firms run on a provincial basis are probably in an even worse state.

If a long-dormant scheme to make SOEs pay proper dividends to their main shareholder, the state, was implemented, it could provide funding for welfare and education but would, obviously, reduce the cash the firms hold and can use to finance themselves or lend out to earn extra revenue. Effective controls on pollution would require additional spending by factories, while a more independent legal system would expose companies to greater external scrutiny and the need for more accountability. Moreover, the end of the *hukou* household registration system would increase the bargaining power of migrant workers.

The reluctance of central and local authorities to take the risks that come with reform has exacerbated the problem. If Xi Jinping and his colleagues had the will and ability to make the changes to propel China into a new stage of development, their task would be made that much tougher by the 'lost decade' under Hu and Wen. The lack of significant action between 2002 and 2012 (except for lifting the farm tax to help the rural world in 2005) may have been understandable politically given the boost of joining the World Trade Organization in 2001 and the exuberance that reigned as the PRC seemed to have a one-way ticket to growth and prosperity. But the story since the boom slowed down in 2008 shows that the economic model needs restructuring. The problem here is one of skills and standards.

The roadmap set in the Five-Year Plan for 2011–15 provided for industry to move up the value chain and for rebalancing towards consumption away from investment and exports as a growth driver. That was eminently sensible, but there were serious snags. The policy adopted in the summer of 2010 was to raise consumption by increasing wages, with instructions to the monopoly trade union to stop acting as an agent of management, as in the past, and to go to bat for workers. The result was substantial pay rises: the minimum wage in some industries almost doubled in four years. But demand continued to rise at roughly the previous level. The next plan, adopted in 2016, offered the same medicine, but aroused doubts about its implementation given the past record.

One major reason was simple: in the absence of a proper health service, with poor public education standards and low pensions, people continue to save in case they fall ill, to pay for private education and for their old age. Health insurance has been extended to 90 per cent of the population, but it provides funding for only three days in hospitals which are known to eject patients with terminal illnesses who cannot pay for treatment and which rely on sales of expensive drugs for their revenue. Other seriously ill people simply do not bother to enrol for care. A study published in 2013 reported that illness eats up 40 per cent of the annual disposable income of rural residents. If government plans for health provision are implemented, this caution will be less evident at the end of the present decade.[9]

But Xi and his team have to deal with the here and now at a time when the challenges are rising for the model on which China runs. Other low-cost countries are providing a growing rivalry in a world export market that is not what it was. Advances in manufacturing technology may restore an edge to developed nations. The shale gas revolution has changed the balance of input costs in the United States. The rebalancing of the global economy from developed to developing worlds has come into question.

Meanwhile, wage rises, increased costs and the higher price of capital are all eating away at the Deng-era combination of cheap labour and cheap savings. The financial system is coming under strain from the huge expansion in lending as the multiplier effect of credit on growth produces diminishing results: while social financing has risen steadily, growth has slowed overall. As the IMF put it in measured language in 2013, the rapid expansion in funding 'raises concerns about the quality of investment and its impact on repayment capacity, especially since a fast-growing share of credit is flowing through less-well supervised parts of the financial system'.[10] Since then, there has been some financial reform, but the Xi administration fell back on credit expansion to limit the drop in growth in 2015–16, and the target for the new Five-Year Plan appears attainable only with a fresh growth in debt and leverage, potentially taking the debt-to-GDP level from the existing 240 per cent through 300 per cent.

In the summer of 2016, the IMF put the debt level of Chinese companies as a whole at 145 per cent of GDP, with state enterprises accounting for just over half the total. The international body called the figure 'very high by any measure' and identified it as 'a key fault line in the Chinese economy'. This constituted 'a serious – and growing – problem that must be addressed immediately and with commitment to serious reforms,' it added. The probability was that at least some SOEs would go into 'zombie' territory where they had to borrow to cover interest on existing loans, producing an upward spiral of borrowing. The central bank said steps would be taken to eliminate loss-making firms and carry out restructuring, but the IMF noted that there had been only 'limited progress' to date.[11]

As for moving up the value chain, there are two major issues connected with this laudable goal. The first is employment. Given the popular image of China as one great workshop, it is easy to ignore the importance of jobs for the regime. George W. Bush records in his memoirs that, when he and Hu Jintao discussed what kept them awake at night, the Chinese leader said it was the need for job creation. Unemployment is certainly higher than the official figure of a little above 4 per cent – it may be double that, plus considerable underemployment particularly in rural areas and the old rust belt of the north-east, though it is not at the level that causes mass social instability. This is something the leadership has to prevent. Hence, for instance, the use of state firms to keep operating plants that retain people in work even when they are not needed, contributing, for instance, to the 30 per cent over-capacity in sectors such as steel and aluminium which produces losses and a glut of loss-making supply to export markets.

Moving up the value chain by introducing more modern technology would, however, lead to fewer jobs. Already, smaller private sector manufacturers say they are reacting to higher wages by installing more machines to take the place of human hands. If that continues, two core objectives of government and Party policy – to give China a more advanced industrial machine and to preserve jobs – must come into conflict. The only hope would lie in the decline in the number of entrants into the labour force as falling fertility and the one-child policy change the demographics. That would be a happy conjunction of circumstances but there is no guar-antee it will happen – or, if it does, that it will be a smooth process.

The other big snag is the skills gap and the weak-ness of regulation to ensure that more advanced products are safe and properly maintained. Coal mine and factory accidents and big explosions and fires in plants in urban areas provide recurrent reminders of the dangers of lax safety standards, but now new problems are becoming apparent with modernization. The crash of two high-speed trains in eastern China in 2011 was a stark reminder that, while the PRC can buy or copy foreign technology, it also has to be able to operate it safely.

When it comes to the innovation that Xi insists is needed, the PRC story is far from replicating the far-off days when China provided the world with everything from industrial innovations to the wheelbarrow and playing cards. The high volume of patent applications is the result of official encouragement rather than of real innovation. China is, in general, good at applying the inventions of others. While its patent office became the busiest in the world in 2011, with slightly more applications than in the United States, the vast majority involved small changes to existing products and the PRC ranked 13th in the world when it came to international patents. Very few Chinese patent applications are also lodged abroad, compared with 40 per cent of those in Europe and 27 per cent of those in America, indicating that the Chinese ones are of limited and national scope.[12]

China has enormous ecommerce companies: Alibaba operates the world's biggest online marketplace for trade between firms, for example – but most mirror originators in the United States. Huawei has developed innovative telecommunications systems that spread globally when not blocked by political fears, but progress in advanced sectors usually depends heavily on imported technology. The efficiency of SOEs is affected by their wider obligations to maintain employment, provide welfare and form part of a politically directed system in which a top manager may be switched to run a province or assume a Party post. Foreign visitors say they meet 'some really smart' managers in the PRC; the problem is that they may be working in a business context which is often short-term or conditioned by political and other external considerations.

Li Keqiang has shown himself aware of the limits of state direction. 'If we place excessive reliance on government steering and policy leverage to stimulate growth, that will be difficult to sustain and could even produce new problems and risks,' he said after becoming Prime Minister in 2013. He stressed the need for the state to retreat in favour of the market's ability to create more evenly distributed wealth and proposed to reduce administrative approval procedures. At the same time, the planning agency, the National Development and Reform Commission (NDRC), laid out plans for gradual liberalization of interest rates and 'promoting the effective entry of private capital into finance, energy, railways, telecommunications and other spheres', with foreign investors gaining greater access to finance, logistics and health care. Moreover, the biggest SOEs were instructed to raise profit growth by at least 10 per cent. Three years later, the results were not apparent as up to half of the state companies were reporting losses, often increased by their high levels of debt.

There is a clear need for a radical attack on the over-capacity built up in the boom days for exports that was fuelled by the easy money available from the end of 2008. The winter of 2015–16 brought a stream of exhortations from the top for the adoption of supply-side economics to streamline sectors such as steel, where there is 30 per cent more capacity than needed. But the rhetoric ran slap into the dangers to stability and regime popularity that would stem from large-scale layoffs – a particular problem in the heavy industry region of the north-east, which was already in recession.

The initial measures that were announced looked quite timid: Reaganite/Thatcherite supply-side policies but with limiting Chinese characteristics. Moreover, there was no guarantee that even that level of change would be carried out: the first steel industry consolidation plan drawn up in the mid-1990s had still not been fully implemented and companies announced plans for new plants even as Beijing was calling for reductions in output. Local and political considerations stand in the way of economic efficiency in a system in which the Communist Party and its cadres at all levels outgun government officials and corporate managers, as shown in the case of the steel mill mentioned above. It appeared that the big state banks would be required to issue yet more loans to cushion the impact of capacity reductions and to avoid company failures creating unacceptable levels of unemployment.

As he approached the long run-up to the 2017 Communist Party Congress, Xi Jinping was clearly torn. He saw the need for modernization and reform, but hesitated to abandon the old mantra of growth that had done so much for the Party, whose strengthening was his bottom line. By then, the guessing game among China watchers was not whether the growth data was over-stated but by how much: was it one or two percentage points below the official 7 per cent, as seemed most likely; was expansion really running at half the official rate, as some economists argued; or was it even close to zero, as a few bears posited? Given the uncertainty about the official figures, nobody could really know, but the projections behind forecasts of global supremacy looked increasingly dubious as the economy showed its growing complexity and efforts at its political direction ran into fresh obstacles that raised new challenges to the Party's basic claim to rule.

Reform was not dropped altogether, but the signals from the top were extremely confused – and confusing to those who had to implement shifting policies. An interview with 'an authoritative figure' in the main Communist newspaper, the *People's Daily*, in the spring of 2016 reflected frustration at the slow pace of modernization and the reliance on debt, which the article warned could lead to a systemic financial crisis. But this was followed the next day by the reprint of a speech by Xi which brushed aside such problems.[13] The conflicting signals appeared to reflect a lack of clear decision-making at the top. Despite warnings of the dangerous level of debt, the Five-Year Plan adopted in March 2016 set an annual growth target of 6.5 per cent, which could only be achieved by yet more leverage. To take another example, a leadership conference at the end of 2015 accepted supply-side economics to eliminate excess capacity, but the Finance Minister then dismissed concerns on this score as 'hype'.[14]

Many of the economic challenges facing the PRC are to be expected in a massive, complex country in the fourth decade of a process of breakneck growth.

This in no way gainsays the progress that has been achieved, but calls for a degree of realism about China's prospects of dominating the globe. That is all the more necessary given the evolution of society, threats to the quality of life and the gulf between the rulers and the PRC's 1.3 billion citizens, as we will now see.

4

The Why Questions

Beside the political and economic challenges the PRC faces lies a complex nexus of social issues which may be the greatest test of Xi Jinping and his colleagues and of the system over which they preside. The ingredients range from wealth disparities to corruption, from the trust deficit to the impact of pollution and recurrent food safety scandals. Taken together they constitute different kinds of 'why' questions about China. Why has the priority been so overwhelmingly on building hardware rather than improving the quality of life? Why have the benefits of material progress not been shared more equitably? Why can the state, which claims such power, not guarantee such basic elements as clean water, trustworthy food and legal protection? Why is the political focus on preserving the system rather than encouraging greater public participation? Why is there so much corner-cutting and such a lack of common trust between rulers and ruled?

The Chinese may have more reverence for the state than is common in the West, but that tradition is based on the bargain that the state will act as protector, and the PRC has not been doing a great job in this respect. The regime faces no threat of being overthrown, but there is a very real danger that it may lose public respect as merely making money becomes less of a priority among the 400 million or so people whose incomes give them time to wonder why such basic livelihood matters are not addressed more effectively, their concerns spread by social media and greater individual liberty.

Still, money remains at the core of the way China works today. This is reflected in the popularity of the *Tiny Times* films (2013–14), which track the lives of four free-spending fashionable young women in Shanghai who make a point of spending all their earnings by the end of each month. The Confucian disdain for the merchant class has little purchase on those driving the economy, producing a fundamental problem for observers who see the sage's teachings as constituting a major element in propelling the PRC to global dominance. Materialism unleashes aspirations and behaviour patterns at odds with the official ethos. Money-making breeds individualism. The human factor has thus become of greater importance than in the days when emperors or revolutionary leaders could regard the Chinese as grains of sand or numbers subject to the will of those in power.

While this is most apparent among the middle class, it is also detectable in the industrial work-force, with a rising pattern of strikes and wage pressure. The monopoly All-China Federation of Trade Unions, which has traditionally acted as an arm of the regime and of management, is under pressure from workers who want to exercise their rights. Second-generation migrants and young women are less willing to be human components on the assembly line, bereft of rights in their adopted urban homes. This increasing militancy was evident in 2016 when unemployed workers at heavy industrial plants closed down in northern China took to the streets to protest. Staff at public sector enterprises regard being laid off as a betrayal of an implicit bargain with the state guaranteeing them lifetime employment, welfare benefits and housing.

While telling pollsters of their pride in the nation's progress, people have been unhappy for some years with the scale of inequalities spawned by the way China has grown. This is not resentment at wealth appreciation as such; rather it is a matter of unhappiness that some have used their positions or illicit methods to accumulate wealth without any control by the authorities – and with the way in which hundreds of millions have been left behind. A Pew Institute poll in 2012 found that 44 per cent of those questioned thought the rich–poor gap was 'a very serious problem' and another 40 per cent saw it as 'at least a moderately big problem'. Eighty-one per cent agreed that 'the rich just get richer while the poor get poorer'.[1] Hence the grassroots popularity of the anti-corruption drive Xi launched on taking the Communist Party helm, which has brought approval from, for example, Beijing butchers who no longer have to give choice cuts of meat free to the police.

The popular anger at corruption which had welled up in the Jiang–Hu era was one of a raft of concerns Chinese expressed to poll-takers which seem, at first sight, to contradict the high levels of approval for their country's economic progress and the performance of the central government. What we have here is top-line satisfaction with the way the PRC has evolved in the last three decades, but, below this, a range of everyday complaints on specific issues such as land requisitioning by local government without adequate compensation, police misbehaviour, corruption and pollution. Local officials get low ratings in keeping with the way in which, in imperial times, people complained about oppressive, grasping local magistrates while venerating the man on the Dragon Throne. Petitioners still travel to Beijing during the annual plenary session of the legislature to try to get satisfaction, even if they are often rounded up by thugs, put into 'black jails' and shipped back home.

Discontent has been building up steadily so far this century. A Gallup poll conducted in 155 countries between 2005 and 2009 to measure satisfaction and happiness levels placed the PRC in 125th place globally. A survey in Party media in 2010 reported that 73.5 per cent of respondents felt 'vulnerable' – nearly half the officials questioned put themselves in that category. The high ratio of property prices to incomes produces constant stress for urban residents on the lower rungs of the real estate ladder in a society where owning your home is an essential mark of success.

The Blue Book of China's Society for 2011, compiled by the Chinese Academy of Social Sciences, reported declining levels of job satisfaction and falling confidence in social welfare. The White Book of Happiness of Middle-Class Families, which surveyed 100,000 people from 35 cities, found that more than half those questioned said they were not happy. A questionnaire in late 2009 asked academics, Party cadres and the general public to name the biggest problems China would face in the coming decade. Corruption and the wealth divide headed the responses, followed by 'a crisis of trust and loss of moral standards'. When the Party newspaper, the *People's Daily*, opened an online poll on Xi Jinping's China Dream, 70 per cent swiftly expressed disapproval, and the site was closed.

Any one survey may be questioned, but such a mass of evidence points to problems at the heart of the People's Republic and where it is headed which reach beyond conventional politics and economics and look like blind-siding the regime's levers of power and authority.

To start with, there is the looming demographic crisis already mentioned. Average births per woman this century have been 1.6 in the PRC, 2.1 in the United States and 2.7 in India. Furthermore, the Chinese Health Ministry says doctors have performed more than 330 million abortions since 1971.

In 2012, the size of the working population fell for the first time under Communist rule as China reached the Lewis Turning Point where the 'demographic dividend' starts to erode. Forecasts of the drop in the number of people aged between 15 and 64 range around 40 million between 2014 and 2030. Meanwhile, life expectancy has risen to an average of 73.5 years. The number of people aged over 60 in 2013 stood at 185 million, or 15 per cent of the population, and will go to 487 million by 2053 according to the China National Committee on Ageing. While the United States and India grow younger, China may become old before it gets rich as its younger generation grapples with the 1:2:4 ratio by which each worker has to support two parents and four grandparents.[2]

Nearly a quarter of China's elderly are below the poverty line. The pension system covers only about 20 per cent of living expenses. Beijing has only three beds in social welfare homes for every 100 old people. The impact of weak health provision is felt most by the old. Polls report 40 per cent of elderly people living in cities saying that they suffer from depression. Family cohesion seems to be fraying: one study showed almost half China's old folk living alone or looking after grandchildren while the parents were far away as migrant workers.[3]

Rural China is full of villages populated by the elderly and infants, the rest of the original inhabitants having gone to work in cities. A survey in Guangdong showed that a quarter of old people received only one visit a year from their children;

three-quarters of those questioned said they longed for more moral support from their offspring. A law was introduced in 2013 ordering children to visit their parents and 'never neglect or snub elderly people'. What does the need for legislation say about the piety towards elders supposedly inherent in China's civilization?

With the demographic shift, China has acquired a serious gender imbalance as parents abort female foetuses or abandon female babies. Males are regarded as being more likely to be able to support their parents and they alone can pay homage to ancestors and ensure that the family lineage is preserved. By 2014, China had 33 million more men than women; that year, according to official figures, 114 boys were born for every 100 girls.[4] This shortage of young women of marriageable age has led to what is known as the 'bride price' in the form of a lavish dowry from the groom. Such 'male bulges' have been linked by some historians to imperial expansion by European powers after 1500 and Japan after 1914. So we have the prospect of a China powered by a testosterone rush, coming at a time when the growth of universities has resulted in millions of unemployed but educated young men.

Environmental damage is dragging down GDP growth as well as harming people's lives and their surroundings. Though there are strict ecological protection laws, they are poorly implemented. Environment Ministry offices across the country are part of local governments which may have interests in polluting factories. A coal power plant opens on average every 10 days. Sulphur from diesel trucks is more than 20 times the level in the West. Serious air pollution – the airpocalypse – regularly envelops Beijing and other major cities in northern China with toxic smog containing particulate matter 40 times the maximum level regarded as safe by the World Health Organization.

While the government has announced major initiatives to try to clean things up, outdoor air pollution is estimated to contribute to 1.2 million premature deaths a year, and a study published in 2013 found that it reduced the life expectancy of inhabitants of northern cities by 5.5 years.[5] That is without taking into account heavy cigarette smoking, which kills 2,000 people a day and could produce an annual death toll of 2 million by 2025.

In addition to the water shortage in the north, water quality is low owing to industrial waste and the flow of fertilizers and pesticides from fields. There are some 10,000 petrochemical plants along the Yangtze and 4,000 on the Yellow River. Up to half China's rivers are reported seriously polluted, with anywhere from 20 to 40 per cent so toxic that contact with their water is considered dangerous. A survey showed that a quarter of 60 lakes and reservoirs which were inspected had excessive amounts of algae. Waste disposal has seriously affected the sea off the PRC. A 2012 report by the Land Ministry found that of 4,929 groundwater monitoring sites across the country, 41 per cent had poor water quality and almost 17 per cent had extremely poor water quality, containing levels of iron, manganese, fluoride, nitrites, nitrates, ammonium and heavy metals exceeding safe limits. The resulting annual human toll is put at 60,000 premature deaths. A report in 2016 said 80 per cent of water in China was unsafe to drink.[6]

The Three Gorges Dam, touted as the biggest project on earth when completed in 2006, is subject to major questioning – over its cost, the 1.3 million people displaced from their homes, its effect on the flow of the Yangtze River and downstream farming, and the creation of what one monitoring group calls 'a festering bog of effluent, silt, industrial pollutants and rubbish' stretching for more than a hundred miles up-river.[7]

Heavy metal discharges from smelters and factories cause cancer and dangerously high levels of lead in blood. Pollution is the main cause of the doubling of the birth-defect rate in Beijing this century. The number of asbestos-related deaths is put at anywhere from 15,000 to 40,000 a year. Solar panel manufacturing has produced lakes of toxic slurry. Recycling of electronic parts imported from the rich world has created villages surrounded by a wasteland of corroded circuit boards, mobile telephone cases and graphic cards stripped of their chips.[8]

Lack of food safety shows itself in dramatic cases such as milk laced with the dangerous chemical melamine to boost its protein count. In 2008, contaminated baby formula affected 300,000 children, of whom 54,000 were treated in hospital and six died; similar cases have surfaced subsequently. Parents who can afford to do so stock up on milk powder for their young infants when they travel outside the mainland; so much so that shops in London and Hong Kong introduced rationing of such products.

Putrid meat is sold after being treated with chemicals. A major processing firm was forced to admit in 2011 that a subsidiary had used pork from pigs fed with the growth enhancer clenbuterol, which can cause serious illness in humans (its use was subsequently banned). Two years later, more than 16,000 carcasses of diseased pigs floated through Shanghai down a tributary of the Huangpu River from farms in Zhejiang Province while, elsewhere in the same region, rat meat was dressed up to be sold as mutton. An outbreak of drug-resistant bird flu killed 36 people in the first half of 2013. A big-selling brand of bottled water, meanwhile, was found to have arsenic levels far beyond benchmark safety standards. Even China's staple food is not immune from contamination. As a result of industrial waste and poor-quality fertilizers, the Food and Drug Administration in the huge southern city of Guangzhou reported in 2013 that 44 per cent of rice samples contained dangerously high amounts of cadmium, which can cause cancer and kidney failure. Researchers in Nanjing said that 10 per cent of the national rice crop is contaminated.[9]

China's safety fault lines stretch from toys containing lead paint to transport. In the summer of 2016, school running tracks made of unchecked industrial waste caused coughing fits, nose bleeds and headaches among children using them. The nuclear industry has only a fraction of the supervisory staff it will need if expansion plans are realized. An investigation of Chinese airlines in 2010 found that they employed more than 200 pilots with fake qualifications. In 2015, 23,500 industrial accidents took 14,136 lives, by the official count. Though closures of unsafe private diggings have reduced the toll, mining remains a dangerous occupation. In 2014, the last year for which official data were released, 931 coal workers died underground. In the spring of 2013, 83 copper miners were killed in a landslide in Tibet amid allegations of lack of safety precautions. That May, a fire in a poultry slaughterhouse in northern China killed 119 people inside, largely because the doors had been locked from the outside to prevent them leaving their work stations during their shifts. Two years later, 179 people were killed and nearly 800 injured by explosions of dangerous chemicals at a storage site in the port city of Tianjin, where safety precautions were lax and officials appeared to have turned a blind eye. Failure to carry out flood-protection work also contributed to the deaths of more than 200 people on the central stretch of the Yangtze River in 2016.

There is a serious shortage of qualified managers. John Quelch, former Dean of the London Business School, who was appointed to head the China Europe International Business School in Shanghai, speaks of managers who believe 'We can do everything',[10] which could lead to risky hubris – a sobering issue when the PRC wants to move up the technological chain with its complex systems. The high-speed train crash in eastern China in 2011 was such a shock because it punctured the idea that the PRC could do anything it liked faster and bigger than any other nation and exposed the management weaknesses in the runaway rail project.

Similar problems were certainly present in now-developed nations as they grew. But they take on an acute character in today's China precisely because of its global importance and what they say about national priorities. The PRC can put on the mega-show of the 2008 Olympics and build a high-speed train network from nothing, airports that put the rest of the world to shame, multi-lane highways and forests of tower blocks. But its pollution gets worse and worse, and regulation remains weak, whatever the rules say and despite budgeted spending of $375 billion on environmental protection and energy conservation between 2010 and 2015. All too often, there is a lack of transparency over the risk to citizens: ministerial inquiries into soil pollution, for instance, are classified as state secrets. Courts are weak and may declare themselves unqualified to deal with cases where local interests are the defend-ants. For factory owners, paying the low fines is cheaper than installing clean equipment. Knowing that their careers are tied to economic growth, local officials have allowed polluting factories to get away with it to boost GDP numbers.

As Xi Jinping acknowledged, graft had become endemic throughout the system as money was diverted from its intended destination to enrich officials and their associates. *The Economist* calculated in 2016 that the PRC (including Hong Kong) had the largest concentration of 'crony wealth' in the world, at $360 billion (though it ranked only 11th when such accretion was set against GDP).[11] An earthquake in Sichuan in 2008 killed 5,000 children in schools which had been poorly built as functionaries squirrelled away the cash which should have gone to put up sturdy buildings. Contractors bidding for public works projects regularly include a provision for bribes in their calculations. A prominent property developer complains that if one gets rich in China it is assumed that one must be corrupt.

Or, at a mundane level, take the case of a Beijing private school where the principal insisted on having an unnecessary ornate gateway built instead of buying much-needed gymnasium equipment and musical instruments. A mother with a child at the school smiles as she says she understands that the school head can expect under-the-counter payments from construction companies but not from sellers of vaulting horses or violins. When a reporter for *Southern Metropolitan News* asked primary school pupils what they wanted to be when they grew up, most gave the usual reply of sports star, rich business person or famous performer. One girl said she would like to be an official. What kind of official, the reporter asked. A corrupt official because they have all the nice things, came the reply.[12]

The Railways Minister, Liu Zhijun, who ran the high-speed rail programme which involved spending of Rmb1.98 trillion (US$320 billion) until he was brought down in 2011 (before the high-speed train crash), was handed a suspended death sentence for raking in Rmb64.6 million, while media reports said a businesswoman who acted as go-between with major firms netted Rmb2.4 billion (US$390 million); she also supplied Liu with mistresses and helped get lenient treatment for his brother when he was accused of plotting the murder of a rival.

So Xi was on firm ground when his war on corruption began by pulling in a deputy director of the main national planning commission, a former Vice-President of a major state bank and a deputy provincial Party Secretary as well as lesser fry. Half-a-dozen PLA generals, both retired and serving, have been punished for accepting bribes or trading in military assets. Other officers were told to stop selling military numberplates that ensure police do not stop cars carrying them. Delegates to the annual plenary session of the two houses of China's legislature in 2013 left their high-end fashion accoutrements at home and, in the words of one, went for 'family-style meals. No shark's fin or fancy dishes.'[13]

The campaign had an undoubted effect. However, it contributed to slower than expected growth in early 2013 as officials held back from launching projects which could expose them. It also aroused a degree of cynicism given the extent of corruption in the system. If they were so guilty, how had Bo Xilai and Zhou Yonghang got away with it for so long and been hailed as important public figures? – people asked. Since the Discipline Commission could strike where it wanted, who was safe and what recourse was there if one was wrongly accused? Better to hunker down and take no risks. And what of the relatives of Xi and Wen Jiabao, whom investigations by Bloomberg and the *New York Times* showed had amassed assets of $376 million and $2.7 billion respectively?[14]

The result is a pervasive trust deficit in a society where deception is rife. Good Samaritans have found themselves successfully sued by those they went to help on the grounds that they must have had an ulterior motive; the Health Ministry was moved to issue a booklet advising the public not to rush to help accident victims. Even the Red Cross

Society of China has been hit over discrepancies in figures for sums collected and disbursed for victims of an earthquake in Sichuan in 2013, setting off a storm of Internet anger. This came after an episode in which a woman who claimed to work for the Red Cross flaunted her wealth, including a Maserati and Hermès handbags, in online postings; it turned out to be a hoax, but it was revealing that a lot of people had believed a charity worker could use public contributions in such a way. The only true fact on the television news put out by the state CCTV station is the date, jokes author Yan Lianke.[15]

The main Shanghai football club was stripped of its league title and fined for match fixing. A zoo in Henan which sent its African lion away for breeding simply substituted a Tibetan mastiff, which, however, gave the game away by barking. Cheating has become so endemic that in one city where the authorities imposed controls on final examinations, girls were checked to see whether they had concealed devices in their brassières to enable them to receive answers to the questions, a measure that caused their parents to mob the schools in protest. People remember how the authorities tried to cover up the outbreak of Severe Acute Respiratory Syndrome (SARS) early this century, the fumbling reaction to the subsequent outbreak of Avian Flu, and how officials connived at contaminated-blood collection in Henan, which may have infected as many as 100,000 when Li Keqiang was the provincial Governor.

Counterfeiting has become a hallmark of China. Eighty per cent of fake goods seized by US and European Union customs originate in the PRC. As well as foreign luxury items, rip-offs occur in domestic products, including medicines, while phoney colleges with names like foreign universities sell bogus diplomas, some held by officials. Jack Ma, Chairman of the huge Alibaba ecommerce group, claimed in a speech in the summer of 2016 that fake goods were often superior to branded names, and at a lower price.[16] But foreign companies continue to struggle under inadequate respect for intellectual property in the PRC, which can reach the point where Chinese firms successfully argue that overseas products should be banned because they are too like their mainland imitators.

Even sources of China's pride and joy have their hollow aspects. At the opening of the Beijing Olympics, the girl singer was dubbed since the real performer was regarded as insufficiently good-looking and all the 56 children who paraded as representatives of ethnic minorities were Han dressed in colourful disguise.

The lack of confidence contributes to a propensity to take direct action in the absence of legal recourse or responsive, accountable local authorities. Social media have facilitated attacks on wayward and corrupt officials, leading in some cases to sanctions. There are estimated to be between 150,000 and 180,000 popular protests each year. Many are peaceful, but some escalate into considerable violence, with crowds of 10,000 or more attacking government buildings and torching police cars. There are also recurrent dramatic acts by individuals who have reached the far borders of frustration, such as the businessman in eastern China who set off three explosions at government offices in his home town after his house was demolished in a road project, or the unemployed man fed up with his lot in life who detonated an explosion on a bus in the city of Xiamen which killed 47 people. A man who lost the use of his legs after reportedly being beaten by security agents detonated an explosive device at Beijing Airport in the summer of 2013, suffering serious injuries; he explained in a blog posting that he was 'almost without hope, petition road endless'.[17]

For millions of Chinese, the recourse has been to turn to Christianity, Buddhism, Daoism and traditional beliefs such as feng shui. The cradle-to-grave 'iron rice bowl' that existed before economic reforms may have been a draconian form of social organization and delivered poor living standards, but it provided a comfort zone for many. Today, the replacement lies outside the system, sometimes to the regime's extreme displeasure, as with the Falun Gong spiritual movement, which has been relentlessly harassed, or in the continuing conflict with the Vatican over the nomination of bishops. One survey showed that half the county-level officials say they believe in divination, face-reading, astrology or interpretation of dreams.[18]

No wonder that the Politburo focuses on what it calls 'social management', acknowledging that 'this is a time when social contradictions are becoming conspicuous in our country'. But the response, so far at least, is inadequate and takes some very knee-jerk forms. The budget for internal security has been increased steeply but the official reply to protests has often been to take the course of least resistance, especially when they are mounted by the middle class, which the leadership wants to keep on side; thus, the authorities in Shanghai, Xiamen on the east coast, Guangdong in the south, Dalian in the north-east and Yunnan in the south-west all cancelled controversial projects or promised reconsideration when people took to the streets. But the regime still reacts with strong-arm tactics when it scents any whiff of a political challenge: an online call in 2011 for a Jasmine Revolution in China similar to those in Arab nations brought out only a tiny handful of people but sparked a huge police presence and the hasty removal of a web posting of Hu Jintao singing a folk song about the flower, just as photographs of Xi holding his umbrella in a rainstorm were taken down when Hong Kong protesters adopted that old Chinese invention as their symbol.

Where do politics stop in China? Consultative Leninism, as this system is sometimes described, is an oxymoron since the Party reserves to itself the right to all decision-making; consultation, in the form of talking to protesters, comes only after the fact. The arbitrary nature of the system remains unaltered. Measures are decided in a closed process without significant public involvement. The enclosed nature of the regime radiates all the way down from the top. The 2012 Party Congress was a prime example of back-room politics with jockeying for position and old power brokers led by Jiang Zemin wheeling themselves out to assert their influence, while the 2017 Congress promises to be an exercise in personal authority by Xi.

The result is the perpetuation of power for the Party State all the way from the leadership compound beside the Forbidden City to Party officials in far-off provinces. As society evolves, it becomes increasingly difficult for the authorities and the regime they represent to engage with the people at large. Though they seek information on popular sentiment through frequent opinion surveys, the combination of the size and complexity of the PRC with the omnipotent claims of its ruling apparatus and the lack of space for adaptation of the basic structure produces a growing disconnect between the Party State and its citizens. The system will not implode or explode politically any more than it will collapse economically. But respect for the way the country is run weakens with each food scandal, each day when inhabitants of the capital fear for their lungs, each corruption case, each dent in Xi's China Dream.

5

China Will Not Dominate the 21st Century

The challenges China faces are perfectly normal for a country that has come so far, so fast, but they provide a powerful argument against being swept away by Sinomania[1] based on a combination of ancient civilizational claims and crude GDP numbers. China's future involves an array of more subtle factors. As one chairman of a large SOE noted privately in 2016, the trouble is that everything is so interconnected by the Party State that, if one element is disturbed, it risks setting off repercussions through the system. To which one may add that the circuit breakers are too weak, the omnipotence of the monopoly political movement too great.

Extrapolation from the last three decades is misleading because it does not take into account the relative simplicity of the first stage of economic growth and the increasing complexity of the second lap. It also assumes that Beijing wants domination and that the United States is set on a course of decline. But as Lee Kuan Yew of Singapore noted, 'The Chinese are in no hurry to displace the US as the Number 1 power in the world and to carry the burden that is part and parcel of that position.'[2]

Nor do their neighbours wish for such an evolution. A visit by President Obama to Vietnam in 2016, during which the two former enemies agreed to move relations forward and the United States concluded contracts to sell weapons to Hanoi, was a dramatic reflection of how the regional dynamics operate, given fear of China's expansion. The sweeping victory of the DPP party in the 2016 presidential and parliamentary elections in Taiwan showed how deep-seated is suspicion of the mainland on the island, which Beijing is committed to recover, while the abduction of Hong Kong booksellers who published volumes the PRC disliked has raised fears of heightened intervention in the former British colony. There is, thus, a considerable disconnect between the friendly reception China gets for its largesse and the degree of caution Asian countries feel about drawing too close to the Great Dragon.

When it comes to the comparison with the post-1945 superpower, there is, on the one hand, the

United States, a country with the world's biggest economy, which is home to all of the 10 largest global companies by market value, the leading source of technical innovation, with treaty allies stretching from Japan to Western Europe, Latin America and Australia – many of them rich, some still growing and three of them in China's East Asian neighbourhood. Accounting for 39 per cent of global military spending, America enjoys enormous preponderance in weapons systems, most of the world's top universities, a reasonably young population, and far-reaching environmental and safety regulations, and, with tracking, it may even be on the brink of an energy revolution with major economic effects. It has a functioning, if imperfect, legal system, free media and global cultural appeal. Its political system can be dysfunctional and jarring, as in the logjam over government spending and the budget in 2013 and the irruption of Donald Trump into the 2016 presidential contest, but it provides alternatives and safety valves, and much of its capacity for self-regeneration exists outside the Washington Beltway.

On the other hand there is China, a state with an economy half the size of the United States in nominal terms, ranking 94th globally in purchasing power parity per capita. It has substantial problems of capital misallocation and excess capacity, weak safety standards, endemic corruption, a dependence on imported resources and foreign advanced technology, plus a weak record in innovation and a reliance on fixed-asset investments backed by pump-priming credit measures that have sent the debt-to-GDP ratio to 250 per cent. As for improvements in the quality of air, water and soil, progress has been slow, and an estimate in 2016 was that the cost of reaching pollution-reduction targets would be $1 trillion.[3] The PRC's financial system is fragile, hemmed in with controls in a network of state institutions. China may possess foreign exchange reserves of more than $3 trillion, but it cannot use the money for domestic purposes because of its financial controls and for fear of setting off a slump in the value of its dollar assets that would undermine this treasure trove.

Though rising fast, military spending amounts to only a quarter of that of the United States. The PRC has 22,000 kilometres of borders with 14 states, some of them potentially or actually unstable, some home to Islamist extremists. The ruling party jealously guards its political control, using repressive means when necessary and wielding the law as a legalist instrument to buttress its rule. Its population is ageing and it faces a mounting range of other social problems. Its army and security apparatus impose Chinese rule on the two huge and recurrently restive territories of Tibet and Xinjiang. Among the permanent members of the Security Council, it is, as noted in Chapter 1, the biggest contributor of non-combat personnel to UN peace-keeping forces and, in 2013, agreed to send fighting troops to help maintain order in Mali, but it plays little role in seeking resolution in major global trouble spots. While the PRC has cooperative associations with many countries which value its assistance, its only formal ally is North Korea. Its constant associations tend to be with poor, troubled nations such as Pakistan and Sudan. Moreover, it showed what it thought of international law when it refused to recognize the UN tribunal that ruled on the South China Sea in 2016.

The international record of the United States, from Vietnam through Iraq to Afghanistan, is pitted with failure. But, while China's purchases of raw materials and willingness to accord aid in return without other strings wins plenty of friends, Beijing has not established itself as a geo-political stakeholder commensurate with its economic clout. The PRC unwaveringly insists on its 'core interests', especially in Tibet and Xinjiang, and in the recovery of Taiwan. Retribution is swift for those who transgress: Britain was put into the dog house for more than a year after the Prime Minister, David Cameron, met the Dalai Lama in London in 2012, with ministerial-level visits blocked by Beijing. China brooks no criticism of its human rights record and, again, is ready to take concrete action to show its displeasure; its purchases of Norwegian salmon fell to one-third of the previous level after the dissident Liu Xiaobo was awarded the Nobel Peace Prize in Oslo in 2010. It stresses the importance of non-interference by nations in the affairs of others, but its foreign policy was long largely a matter of resources diplomacy conducted on a bilateral, case-by-case basis.

As the major rising state in a world system constituted by the West after the Second World War and reinforced by the fall of the Soviet Union, the PRC is, by nature, a revisionist power. But this involves a paradox, for its rise has been made possible by the status quo as regards both its trade and its ability to exclude unwanted external influences. Beijing is understandably miffed at the strong US military presence and the 'island chain' of Washington's allies running from Okinawa through Taiwan to the Philippines. Yet the regional security that has underpinned its export growth depends in the end on the presence of the country from the other side of the Pacific. Beijing resents the way in which the operations of international organizations were set before it emerged from the isolation of the Mao era, but it advances few concrete propositions for change. As the British China watcher Guy de Jonquières put it pithily: 'Over the past three decades, China has shown that it can shake the established world order. It has yet to show that it can help shape a future one.'[4] That may be in keeping with the Sino-centric attitude of the dynastic past, but it hardly points to global dominance for the heirs of the Middle Kingdom.

In Asia, Beijing pursues asymmetrical relationships as it seeks to assert itself as top dog, echoing the tributary states system of the imperial era. But, important as their economic ties with the mainland are, its neighbours are none too keen to fall in with China's wishes, and they have the protective umbrella of the United States to encourage resistance. The effect of the PRC's assertive claims to sovereignty over virtually all the 3.5 million square kilometres of the South China Sea and to the uninhabited Senkaku/Diaoyu Islands off Japan has been to drive the other states involved ever deeper into the arms of Washington, as noted earlier. Relations with India, where four-fifths of those polled regard China as a security threat, are scratchy, with a running territorial dispute on the Himalayan frontier and Indian unhappiness about its $40 billion annual trade deficit with the PRC.

Xi Jinping has described Russia and China as 'most important strategic partners' who speak a 'common language', reinforced by big gas deals and infrastructure plans. But relations are watchful, with territorial tensions on their border. Meanwhile the dispute with Japan over the Senkaku/Diaoyu Islands, which reflects a much deeper tussle between the two countries, is not likely to go away since leaders in both Beijing and Tokyo see it as a sop to nationalism.

The key global relationship, between China and the United States, is cool or chilly. Each side knows that it needs the other and has every interest in avoiding the 'Thucydides Trap' whereby a rising power and the ruling state come into conflict, like Athens and Sparta in ancient Greece or Germany and Britain in the early 20th century, though parallels between East Asia and pre-1914 Europe are overdone, if only because of nuclear deterrence.[5] The two great powers remain far apart in basic values – even if human rights are little mentioned in public by US administrations these days. A survey in 2013 showed that the proportion of Americans expressing a positive view of the PRC had slumped from 51 to 37 per cent in two years while Chinese good opinions of the United States fell from 58 to 40 per cent.[6]

When it comes to 'soft power', where admirers expect China's civilizational strengths to make themselves felt, the case for PRC dominance is equally unproven. Yes, there are 700 Confucius Institutes and classrooms round the world teaching Mandarin, while the CCTV state network has opened international operations and *China Daily* publishes editions in Europe, North America, Asia and Africa. But few people choose to adopt the Chinese way of life, or think in a way approved by the leaders in Beijing. A regime which cannot admit to uncomfortable facts in its own history and refuses debate on its assumed truths is hardly in a position to win wide international intellectual support. Despite their country's increased prosperity, plenty of Chinese seek to move abroad. Apart from North America, Australia and New Zealand, around one million Chinese are estimated to have gone to live in Europe this century, whether legally or illegally. Some 80,000 gain US green cards each year and an agency in Beijing charges $15,000 or more to advise the well-off on means of gaining foreign residence status.

For all Xi Jinping's globe-trotting and the PRC's open cheque book, warmth for China seems to be somewhat on the wane, to judge by recent polls. Though some countries wanted to win favour with Beijing, the rush of US allies to join the Asian Infrastructure Bank was mainly a tactical decision to take part in an initiative which might yield them dividends rather than a strategic shift. How much will come in concrete terms of the 'One Belt, One Road' programme remains to be seen; indications in Beijing in 2016 were that many projects were still at the conceptual stage and did not take proper account of the difficulties involved in, say, building a transport corridor and pipeline from a new port in Pakistan through dangerous territory to Xinjiang.

China's higher international profile has, inevitably, opened it up to greater scrutiny, especially in the West. The 2016 US presidential contest was peppered with criticism of the PRC, with Donald Trump proposing a 45 per cent tax on imports from the mainland. In the United Kingdom, David Cameron proclaimed his aim of making his country China's best friend in Europe (a vain hope given the strength of the economic relationship between the PRC and Germany), but one of the first acts of his successor, Theresa May, was to order a review of the two nations' flagship cooperation project, the nuclear power station at Hinckley Point in Somerset. In addition, Queen Elizabeth was caught on camera saying how rude the Chinese leader's entourage was on his state visit to London in 2015. Then, China was blamed for sending up bacon prices in the United Kingdom because of its demand for pork to compensate for the impact of flooding on its pig farms in the summer of 2016. There are also complaints about working practices at Chinese-operated enterprises in Africa, while Beijing's cultivation of natural resources producers like Venezuela, Zambia and Zimbabwe have run into domestic problems there and President Jacob Zuma of South Africa has spoken of trade patterns that are 'unsustainable in the long term'.

The PRC remains, by its nature, a dependent power, constrained by its reliance on imports of minerals, oil, gas and, in the event of a bad harvest, food or animal feed. This is in striking contrast to the United States in its era of expansion. China has around 20 per cent of the world's population but less than half that much of its arable land and renewable water, and, as we have seen, both these vital resources are under threat.

Despite the headlines about China buying up the world, its major acquisitions outside the raw materials and food industries were limited for a long time, leaving it with a lot of room to catch up in foreign investments. Its efforts to acquire advanced technology have often been blocked by national security considerations. Foreign companies in the PRC, meanwhile, know they need to remain in such a big market but are growing cooler towards increasing investment as they find the playing field tilted against them in a more nationalistic environment.

Enthusiasts for the China model insist that the system is in a constant process of ameliorative change; indeed, the commentator and private equity financier Eric Li goes so far as to suggest that the Communist Party is 'the world's leading expert in political reform'.[7] Such a claim is difficult to credit of a ruling organization which is constantly scrabbling to assert its authority and legitimacy. Its leadership faces a classic paradox, as we have seen throughout this book: it needs to reform in order to rule more effectively, but reform brings with it the threat of weakening the system. After a decade in which the status quo was strengthened, the far-reaching repercussions of necessary change would shake the system, in part, and face the leadership with an array of challenges for which it appears to lack sufficient policy tools or implementation expertise.

Above all, the maintenance of control that lies at the core of the Communist Party runs counter to the need to liberalize the economy and society, and, eventually, politics. China finds itself at a watershed in which it needs to change but knows that change will face it with its biggest test since Deng Xiaoping found the way out of the disaster of the Mao era in the late 1970s.

Its current leadership was reminded of the dangers it faced by the circulation at the time of the 2012 Party Congress of a reading list which included Alexis de Tocqueville's account of the fall of the Bourbon monarchy in France at the end of the 18th century. Tocqueville argued that an autocracy is most vulnerable when it starts to reform, with regime change most likely when improved living conditions give people time to think. Following on from that, a commentator in the business magazine *Caixin* noted that 'as a government continues to incite the desire for wealth accumulation, which breeds corruption and saps its moral credibility, prosperity actually plants the seed of the regime's demise'. 'Economic growth,' he continued, 'instead of keeping people content, makes them restive.' Thus the high growth rate, 'long perceived in China as sine qua non for stability, may have the opposite effect. ... Economic progress has lost its magic; equality and justice now matter more. Even the moderates think change must happen to pull China out of stagnation.'[8] Or, as Zhou Qiren, Dean of the National School of Development at Peking

University, has warned: 'Without true reform, even bigger trouble will be waiting. ... The authorities seem to have forgotten that if nothing is to be challenged or reviewed, this will naturally lead to heterodoxy. China is standing before a critical crossroads, where reforms are as difficult as they are necessary. The more that progress is delayed, the harder it becomes.'[9]

China's resentment at being part of a global system whose rules it did not frame is generally underestimated in the West, which set those rules and is happy with them. The belief, in Washington and elsewhere, that all that is required is for the PRC to operate by those standards, as if they had the everlasting sanctity of tablets of global law, is extremely short-sighted. But, equally, Beijing's failure to put forward discussable alternatives risks relegating it to the status of a querulous outsider in a world system it has joined and needs, but with which it has not really engaged beyond short-term advantage. Given China's economic weight and the lasting change it has brought to the international balance, this is potentially very dangerous; the big outsider is never a good factor for others, or, in the end, for itself, and its size and exclusion, real or perceived, can lead to escalating conflict that imperils all.

The result is the watershed which will determine the course the country takes in this decade and beyond. The accumulation of problems listed in this book are, in a sense, hardly surprising given the extent of development and the priorities adopted since 1978, and do not, in themselves, point to the coming collapse of China, given the resources of the Party State.

But they are now piling up in a dangerous fashion and there may not be much time to deal with the combination of pressures. Donald Trump's questioning of the 'One China' policy for relations with the US poses a big foreign policy challenge as Beijing faces the new style in Washington. Decision-making will be difficult for a leadership which has long avoided hard choices and is hemmed in by the cocoon of embedded Party rule. If reform is not undertaken in a far-reaching manner, the PRC will lurch from problem to problem, limiting its future development. If change is grasped, there will be a protracted and difficult transition for the system built up since 1949. Either way, domestic factors will constrain the extension of the country's global influence as the leadership focuses on internal matters. Domination of the 21st century is not in prospect when the prime concern will be to keep the 'China Dream' alive at home.

Further Reading

The case for Chinese global dominance is put most strongly by Martin Jacques in *When China Rules the World* (London: Allen Lane, 2009; second edition, 2012), though the author himself says the 'catchy' title should not be taken too literally. A number of earlier books had charted China's rise, starting almost two decades ago with Jim Rohwer's *Asia Rising* (New York: Simon & Schuster, 1995). The argument for a Chinese crash was first advanced, to my knowledge, by Gordon Chang in *The Coming Collapse of China* (New York: Random House, 2001), though the forecast in the title has not, of course, come to pass. The two sides in the debate on whether the 21st century will belong to China were represented by Niall Ferguson and David Daokui Li (for) and Fareed Zakaria and Henry Kissinger (against) in the Munk Debate in Toronto in 2011 –

the audience voted 62 per cent against the motion (*http://www.munkdebates.com/debates/china*).

Daniel Bell argues the case for meritocracy in *The China Model* (Princeton: Princeton University Press, 2016). David Shambaugh's *China's Future* (Cambridge: Polity, 2016) presents a penetrating analysis of contemporary China, while Xi Jinping's past and early years in power are covered in Willy Wo-lap Lam's *Chinese Politics in the Era of Xi Jinping* (London: Routledge, 2015) and Kerry Brown's *China's CEO* (London: I.B. Tauris, 2016). Minxin Pei's *China's Trapped Transition* (Cambridge, MA: Harvard University Press, 2008) remains highly apposite.

Gideon Rachman provides an excellent, accessible overview of the current impact of Asia's rise on the world in *Easternisation: War and Peace in the Asian Century* (London: Bodley Head, 2016). Stephen G. Brooks and William C. Woolworth provide the argument for continuing US supremacy in their article in the May/June 2016 edition of *Foreign Affairs*, 'The Once and Future Superpower: Why China Won't Overtake the United States'.

Richard McGregor's *The Party* (London: Allen Lane, 2010) gives the best description and analysis of the political system. *Red Capitalism* by Carl Walter and Fraser Howie (Singapore: John

Wiley, 2011) is a penetrating analysis of the financial system. Jonathan Watts provides an excellent survey of the ecological disaster in *When a Billion Chinese Jump* (London: Faber & Faber, 2010). Leslie Chang's *Factory Girls* (London: Picador, 2010) presents superb reportage on migrant workers. Arne Odd Westad's *Restless Empire* (London: Bodley Head, 2012) covers China's relations with the world since 1750, while David Shambaugh's *China Goes Global* (Oxford: Oxford University Press, 2013) presents the PRC as a 'partial power'. Lee Kuan Yew delivers his judgements on China, the United States and the future in interviews with Graham Allison, Robert D. Blackwill and Ali Wyne in *Lee Kuan Yew: The Grand Master's Insights on China, the United States and the World* (Cambridge, MA: MIT Press, 2013). Peter Nolan provides a salutary corrective to the China outward investment story in *Is China Buying the World?* (Cambridge: Polity, 2012).

Ezra Vogel's *Deng Xiaoping and the Transformation of China* (Cambridge, MA: Harvard University Press, 2011) gives a monumental account of the man who changed the world. Frank Dikötter's trilogy *The People's Tragedy* (London: Bloomsbury, 2010–16) lays out in forensic detail the horrific human cost of the Great Helmsman's policies and ambition. Roderick MacFarquhar's three-volume *Origins of the Cultural Revolution* (New York: Columbia University Press, 1974–99) and the following volume with Michael Schoenhals, *Mao's Last Revolution* (Cambridge, MA: Belknap Press, 2008), remain the best account of the politics of that era.

For those in a hurry and seeking expert guidance, Jeffrey Wasserstom's *China in the 21st Century* (Oxford: Oxford University Press, 2010) answers most of the questions people ask about China in 135 pages, while Rana Mitter provides *Modern China: A Very Short Introduction* (Oxford: Oxford University Press, 2008). My own books, *The Penguin History of Modern China* (London: Penguin, 2009; second edition, 2013) and *Tiger Head, Snake Tails: China Today* (London: Simon & Schuster, updated paperback edition, 2013), cover China past and present.

Notes

Chapter 1 The China Dream

1 Poverty, World Bank data: *http://povertydata.world-bank.org/poverty/home/*; space: *http://www.bbc.co.uk/news/world-asia-china-36630768?utm*.

2 See Martin Jacques, *When China Rules the World* (London: Allen Lane, 2009; second edition, 2012); Daniel Bell, *The China Model* (Princeton: Princeton University Press, 2016). Niall Ferguson: *http://www.munkdebates.com/debates/china*.

3 European Chamber of Commerce paper, Beijing, 7 June 2016: *http://uk.reuters.com/article/us-china-eu-business-idUKKCN0YT04Y*.

4 Survey: *Financial Times*, 14 June 2016; universities: *Caixin*, 20 June 2016.

5 For the way the leadership re-creates history to serve its purposes, see Ian Johnson, 'The Presence of the Past – A Coda', in Jeffrey Wasserstrom (ed.),

The Oxford Illustrated History of China (Oxford: Oxford University Press, 2016).

6 *http://southasiaanalysis.org/node/1985*.
7 Private conversation with the author, 2010.
8 *Financial Times*, 18 June 2016.
9 *PLA Daily*, 22 May 2013; Xi press conference, Rancho Mirage, California, 10 June, 2013; military parade commentary, Beijing, 3 September 2015.
10 *http://www.bbc.co.uk/news/world-asia-china-36569710*.
11 Mark Elvin, *The Pattern of the Chinese Past* (Stanford: Stanford University Press, 1973).
12 Henry Kissinger, *China* (London: Penguin, 2012).

Chapter 2 The Price of Politics

1 For Xi's rise and first years in power, see Willy Wo-lap Lam, *Chinese Politics in the Era of Xi Jinping* (London: Routledge, 2015) and Kerry Brown, *China's CEO* (London: I.B. Tauris, 2016).
2 *South China Morning Post*, 30 August 2016.
3 *Economist*, 7 May 2016.
4 For Xi's associates, see Cheng Li's expert analysis in 'Xi Jinping's Inner Circle', Parts 1–5, *China Leadership Monitor* nos 43–7 (Spring 2014–Summer 2015): *http://www.hoover.org/publications/china-leadership-monitor*. For Xi as the embodiment of the Party, see Brown, *China's CEO*, with summary in the Preface, pp. xiv–xv.
5 *PLA Daily*, 22 May 2013.
6 *Financial Times*, 2 June 2016.

7 Economic developments in 2015–16 are dealt with in more detail in the next chapter.

8 Radio Free Asia, 20 June 2016.

9 For the new leadership see *China Leadership Monitor*: *http://www.hoover.org/publications/china-leadership-monitor*.

10 *Le Monde*, 12 May 2013.

11 *Qiushi*, June 2016.

12 Richard McGregor, *The Party* (London: Allen Lane, 2010), p. 1.

13 *People's Daily*, 22 May 2013.

14 *Caixin*, 10 December 2012.

15 *New York Times*, 19 July 2013.

Chapter 3 The Middle Development Trap

I am grateful for ideas in this chapter drawn from discussions over the years with my colleagues at Trusted Sources, especially Bo Zhuang, Larry Brainard and Trey McArver.

1 *http://www.worldbank.org/en/news/press-release/2012/02/27/china-case-for-change-on-road-t-030*.

2 *Neue Zürcher Zeitung*, 24 May 2013.

3 *The Economist*, 19 May 2005.

4 IMF: *http://www.imf.org/external/np/sec/pr/2013/pr13192.htm*; *Financial Times*, 18 July 2013.

5 *Wall Street Journal*, 26 June 2013.

6 *Guardian*, 17 March 2013.

7 *http://news.xinhuanet.com/english/china/2013-07/20/c_132558552.htm?utm_source=Sinocism+News letter&utm_ campaign = 4bf43bd340 - Sinocism07 _*

21_13&utm_medium=email&utm_term=0_171f2
378674bf43bd340-29592865.

8 *Financial Times*, 13 June 2016.

9 China Health and Retirement Longitudinal Survey, 2013.

10 *Financial Times*, 18 July 2013; *Wall Street Journal*, 26 June 2013.

11 *Financial Times*, 13 June 2016.

12 *The Economist*, 5 January 2013.

13 *People's Daily*, 9–10 May 2016.

14 *Financial Times*, 7 June 2016.

Chapter 4 The Why Questions

1 Pew Survey, 22 September 2015: *http://www.pew global.org / 2015 / 09 / 24 / corruption - pollution - in equality-are-top-concerns-in-china/*.

2 China Research Center on Aging, 2013; Poverty line, China Health and Retirement Longitudinal Study, 2013.

3 *South China Morning Post*, 1 June 2013.

4 *Xinhua*, 20 January 2015.

5 Yanzhong Huang, *YaleGlobal*, 6 June 2013; *Proceedings of the National Academy of Sciences*, 2013; *New York Times*, 8 July 2013.

6 *Nature*, 3 July 2013.

7 *http://damsandalternatives.blogspot.co.uk/2013/05/ ft-water-shortages-in-china-and-three.html*.

8 For the origins and costs of the environmental crisis, see Elizabeth Economy, 'The Great Leap Backwards', *Foreign Affairs*, September/October 2007.

9 *Wall Street Journal*, 23 May 2013.
10 *China Daily*, European edition, 19–25 August 2011.
11 *The Economist*, 7 May 2016.
12 *http://chinadigitaltimes.net/2009/09/video-six-years-old-i-want-to-be-a-currupted-official-when-i-grow-up/*.
13 *Wall Street Journal*, 15 March 2013.
14 Bloomberg, 29 June 2012: *http://www.bloomberg.com/news/2012-06-29/xi-jinping-millionaire-relations-reveal-fortunes-of-elite.html*; *New York Times*, 25 October 2012.
15 Yan Lianke, Asia House, London, 21 May 2013.
16 *Financial Times*, 18 June 2016.
17 *New York Times*, 20 July 2013.
18 *New York Times*, 13 May 2013.

Chapter 5 China Will Not Dominate the 21st Century

1 Sinomania is a term coined in the headline for a review of books on China by Perry Anderson in the *London Review of Books*, 28 January 2010.
2 *Lee Kuan Yew: The Grand Master's Insights on China, the United States and the World*, interviews and selections by Graham Allison, Robert D. Blackwill and Ali Wyne (Cambridge, MA: MIT Press, 2013), p. 11.
3 Bloomberg, 7 June 2016: *http://www.bloomberg.com/news/articles/2016-06-07/china-s-cities-need-1-trillion-green-finance-to-cut-pollution*.
4 See *China's Geoeconomic Strategy*, LSE Ideas, June 2012.

5 Graham Allison, *Financial Times*, 22 August 2012.

6 *http://www.pewglobal.org/2013/07/18/global-image-of-the-united-states-and-china/*.

7 *http://www.ted.com/talks/eric_x_li_a_tale_of_two_political_systems.html*. The ensuing debate on democracy, in which Li's arguments are taken to task by Yasheng Huang of the MIT Sloan School of Management, is at *http://blog.ted.com/why-democracy-still-wins-a-critique-of-eric-x-lis-a-tale-of-two-political-systems/*.

8 *Caixin*, 14 September 2012.

9 Real Clear World, 2 July 2013: *http://www.realclearworld.com/articles/2013/07/02/why_real_reform_in_chin_can_no_longer_wait_105293.html*.